the BIBLE
IN 52 WEEKS

the

BIBLE
IN 52 WEEKS

A Yearlong Bible Study for Women

DR. KIMBERLY D. MOORE

CALLISTO PUBLISHING

Art Director: Liz Cosgrove
Art Producer: Samantha Ulban
Editor: Lauren O'Neal
Production Editor: Ruth Sakata Corley

Published by Callisto Publishing LLC C/O Sourcebooks LLC
P.O. Box 4410, Naperville, Illinois 60567-4410
(630) 961-3900
callistopublishing.com

Printed and bound in China.
OGP 26

This book is dedicated
to all of the strong, phenomenal,
fearless women who have
made a difference in my life.
Thank you, one and all.

CONTENTS

INTRODUCTION

I HAVE BEEN INVOLVED IN MINISTRY for as long as I can remember. I was born and raised in the church. I received Jesus Christ as Lord and Savior as a college student and have been serving Him faithfully ever since. Over the years, I've served in various offices and capacities of ministry: Sunday school superintendent and teacher, church musician, choir director, women's ministry leader, Bible study teacher, church administrator, and accountant.

In 1995, I obtained my license to preach the gospel of Jesus Christ, and I was ordained as a minister in a local church in 2001. Later, I became assistant pastor of one of its outreach ministries. I soon enrolled in seminary and attended on a part-time basis for several years until withdrawing in 2008, when I was blessed to be elected as the full-time senior pastor at Emmanuel Missionary Baptist Church in Gastonia, North Carolina.

My election was a historic event in Gaston County. I'm the first woman to serve as a senior pastor in the Gaston County Missionary Baptist Association, and I'm one of very few in the state of North Carolina. Needless to say, there is not enough female representation in church leadership (especially in the Baptist church). This fact stirred the mentor in me, and I started to encourage other women in ministry, sharing the knowledge and principles I have acquired throughout the years.

I am very thankful that God has blessed my life in such an amazing way, and it is my joy to share some thoughts with you now. I've thoroughly enjoyed writing about some of my favorite Bible stories that I believe will give you insight and new revelation.

Oftentimes, we hesitate to read the Bible, because the language can be difficult or it's hard to interpret the meaning of the text. This book is written to help you read, understand, and apply the Bible to your daily life. Many of the biblical quotations I've used throughout are from the New Living Translation and the New King James Version. These translations present scripture in an accessible way that will make reading this book an enjoyable part of your daily routine.

As you read this book alongside the Word of the Lord, I hope you'll be encouraged to be your best self and find some of the answers you've been seeking. As women, sometimes we're the glue that holds everything together. We are the ones who encourage and uplift. We soothe boo-boos and love the hurt away. But who encourages us? Who lifts our spirits and bandages our wounds? It is my prayer that this book will uplift your spirit, draw God's healing into where you're hurting, and remind you how amazing you are.

HOW TO USE THIS BOOK

THIS BOOK WILL HELP YOU read and learn from the entire Bible. If you stay the course, you will have read the entire Bible in a year's time. I want to be sure you get the most out of your time of meditation and study. Too often, we don't complete books of this nature because they aren't as accessible as they should be or we're just too busy. With this book, you'll only need about 15 minutes to complete your daily reading, and it will be time well spent!

It is first important to know the makeup of the Bible. It consists of 66 books: 39 in the Old Testament and 27 in the New Testament. The Old Testament is divided into books of the law, historical writings, books of poetry, and major and minor writings by prophets. The Old Testament contains a wealth of invaluable information and historical records that help us grasp the foundation on which our beliefs are established.

The New Testament is made up of the Gospels, the historical Acts of the Apostles, letters written by the Apostle Paul, several other general letters, and the prophetic book of Revelation. The New Testament brings us hope through Jesus Christ. We are told of His miraculous birth, His influential life on earth, His horrific death, and His redeeming resurrection. We see the formation of the church, and we are trained and equipped for life and ministry so that we may be prepared when the Lord comes back and we can live with Him eternally.

There are many translations of the Bible. Feel free to use the one you're most comfortable with, as this book is written to complement any translation. Choose the one that gives you the most clarity while you're reading. In addition, this book has nothing to do with church preference or denomination—it's all about spending quality time with God through His Word.

WHAT MATERIALS DO I NEED?

This book.

The Bible. Use any version or translation you'd like. You may also benefit from an electronic or audio version that can be downloaded on your phone.

Notebook, journal, or iPad. This will be helpful if you want to take extra notes.

Pen or pencil.

WHAT'S IN THIS BOOK?

This book outlines daily scripture readings for all 52 weeks of the year. You will find suggested readings from the Bible for six days of every week. On the seventh day, you're encouraged to catch up on any readings that you may have missed during the week. Along with the daily readings is a commentary based on one of the week's scripture selections that will help you apply the lessons from the Bible to your everyday life. Following the commentary, you'll find questions to inspire you to think about your own journey, as well as a prayer, a highlighted verse, or action steps for exercising your faith or overcoming an issue you're facing.

You'll be tackling the Bible in very manageable portions. The scripture readings should take 15 to 20 minutes a day. The readings are not in strictly chronological order, which will help you stay motivated as you move through the scriptures. You don't have to wait for months to get to the beauty of the Gospels or the grandeur of the Psalms; they'll pop up at different points throughout the year. You may enjoy the visions of an Old Testament prophet one week and some of Paul's letters to the church the next.

GREAT IN A GROUP OR ON YOUR OWN

One of the great things about studying the Bible is that it can be done alone or in a group setting like a book club or small group at church. This book has a list of questions at the back specifically designed for group discussion (see page 185). You can also use each week's questions to facilitate discussion and share personal stories. Either way, this book will be a jumping-off point for stimulating conversations.

YOU CAN DO IT!

Some people love to read, and others do not. If you don't find reading very enjoyable, try using an audio version of the Bible or reading from a Bible app on your phone. If, for some reason, you get a little behind, don't beat yourself up. Just pick up where you left off and keep going. This book is designed to help you get used to reading and spending time in the Word daily.

You will find that the more time you spend in the Word, the more knowledgeable and equipped you'll become. As you add this book to your daily routine, it is my hope that you'll learn to enjoy spending more time in the Word of God. I believe in you, my sister, and I believe you can accomplish anything. Let's get started!

WEEK 1
THERE'S NOTHING TOO HARD FOR GOD!

DAILY READINGS

Day 1: Genesis 1–4

Day 2: Genesis 5–8

Day 3: Genesis 9–12

Day 4: Genesis 13–15

Day 5: Genesis 16–18

Day 6: Genesis 19–21

Day 7: Catch up on any readings you've missed.

MY PURPOSE IS TO ENCOURAGE the encourager today. While you focus on the needs of those around you, remember that God has not forgotten about you. He hears your prayers and remembers your heart's desires and struggles. He posed a question to Abraham in Genesis 18:14: "Is anything too hard for the Lord?" (NIV). And the answer is that there is absolutely nothing too hard for God. Ephesians 3:20 says that God "is able to do exceedingly abundantly above all that we ask or think, according to the power that works in us" (NKJV). There is nothing you could think of or ask that God cannot do.

In the story of Sarah and Abraham, God told Abraham that He would make him a great nation and from him all the families of the earth would be blessed (Genesis 12:2–3). This promise probably didn't make sense to Abraham at the time, because he and Sarah had no children, and, well into their senior years, they thought they were too old.

In chapter 16, Sarah still hadn't had a child yet, so she took matters into her own hands and decided that Abraham should sleep with her maid, Hagar. Abraham and Hagar had a son named Ishmael. God allowed it, but He did not ordain it. You must be mindful that when it comes to the promises of God, you shouldn't take matters into your own hands.

In chapter 18, God made Abraham and Sarah a specific promise—one that didn't make sense. The odds were against them because of their age; Abraham was 100 and Sarah was 90 years old. By this time, it had been 13 years since God made His original promise in chapter 12, and they had seen no signs of their earlier promise. What do you do when you've waited so long and somebody is telling you that the impossible is still possible? What do you do when the promise just doesn't make sense?

You've got to decide in your heart not to give in to the doubt. I know that's easier said than done. I've had to learn the hard way that doubting hinders the progress to your promise, paralyzes you, and keeps you stagnant. It makes you want to take control rather than trust God with your life. However, when you replace doubt with faith, you give God something to work with.

It's easy to be skeptical when the odds are against you. But I encourage you to trust God to keep His Word. When you replace doubt with faith, trust that God will do His part and release the blessing. You have to believe that there is absolutely nothing too hard for God to do!

POINTS TO PONDER

1. When you were faced with an impossibility, how did you handle it? After this lesson, how will you handle those impossibilities going forward?

_____

_____

_____

2. What has this lesson taught you about your faith?

_____

_____

_____

3. What areas have you discovered where you are strong in faith? What areas have you discovered where your faith needs to be strengthened?

_____

_____

_____

_____

4. After this lesson, what are some impossibilities that you will commit to prayer?

_____

_____

_____

_____

ACTIONS FOR THE WEEK

1. Decide in your heart to think and speak positively, replacing negative words with positive ones.

2. Make a commitment to yourself to intentionally respond to your doubts with declarations of faith.

3. At the end of the week, note how speaking positively into your life has begun to have a good impact on your outlook and ability to trust God.

WEEK 2
GIVING UP IS
NOT AN OPTION

DAILY READINGS

◻ Day 1: Genesis 22–25

◻ Day 2: Genesis 26–29

◻ Day 3: Genesis 30–33

◻ **Day 4: Genesis 34–36**

◻ Day 5: Genesis 37–41

◻ Day 6: Genesis 42–46

◻ Day 7: Catch up on any readings you've missed.

HAVE YOU EVER just wanted to kick yourself for giving up too soon on a goal? For example, maybe you told yourself you didn't have time to go back to school and complete that degree, even though you were only a few credits shy of graduating. I know—life happened. You had financial struggles, were caring for an ailing loved one, or had kids, and you had to put your dreams on the back burner. So you gave up and told yourself that it was just too late for you.

In Genesis 35, Rachel died before reaching her promise. If you've been keeping up with the readings, you know that in Genesis 30, Rachel grieved over the fact that she couldn't have a child. Her sister, Leah, was fruitful, but Rachel was unable to conceive, which caused her much heartache. But God finally blessed Rachel with a son, whom she named Joseph. After experiencing this miracle, she immediately spoke a prophetic word into her own life and said that she would have another son. She had faith that God could do it again.

However, Rachel made a mistake. She didn't have enough faith to put God completely first and stop worshiping idols, and it brought her down. In Genesis 31, she stole her father's idols from his house when she left with Jacob. When her father came looking for the idols, Jacob called for the death of the person who had stolen them, not knowing Rachel was the culprit. She did get pregnant again and began to go into labor—"hard labor," according to Genesis 35:16 (NKJV). But because of the intense labor pain brought on by her disobedience, she died in childbirth. She was so close to her destination, but she died. The baby was successfully delivered. The miracle still came, but Rachel couldn't enjoy the fruit of her labor.

My dear sister, giving up is not an option, no matter how difficult the journey! You have amazing goals and dreams. Please do not let those dreams die. Please know that somebody is waiting on what is to come through you. They are waiting on a mentorship, a book, or a business that has to be birthed through you. So pick those dreams back up, dust them off, and get back on track. You are much closer than you think.

POINTS TO PONDER

1. What goals did you give up on that just seemed too far-fetched?

_____

_____

_____

_____

2. What visions or dreams do you have that you need to pick up and dust off?

_____

_____

_____

_____

3. In this story, Rachel had a midwife who tried to encourage her to hold on to her promise. Who do you know who needs encouragement to hold on? How will you help them?

_____

_____

_____

_____

ACTIONS FOR THE WEEK

1. Take a few minutes three times this week to pray for direction to get your goals back on track.

2. Commit to watching a video or listening to a podcast that will help jump-start your creative juices in your particular area of interest.

3. Put a timeline in place to accomplish some of your goals, one at a time.

4. Share your goals and timeline with someone so they can help keep you accountable.

WEEK 3
EVERYTHING IS PURPOSEFUL

DAILY READINGS

- Day 1: Genesis 47–50
- **Day 2: Exodus 1–3**
- Day 3: Exodus 4–7
- Day 4: Exodus 8–11
- Day 5: Exodus 12–15
- Day 6: Exodus 16–18
- Day 7: Catch up on any readings you've missed.

IN THE SECOND CHAPTER of Exodus, we find the story of the birth of Moses. Pharaoh had issued a decree that all Israelite males be put to death as soon as they were born. Moses's mother wanted to do what any loving mother would do and save her son. She wrapped him up, put him in a basket made of bulrushes, and strategically placed him in the river so he'd end up in the right hands. That day, Pharaoh's daughter was bathing in those same waters and sent her maid to retrieve the basket she saw floating in the reeds. She felt sorry for the child, correctly assuming he was one of the Hebrew babies. Moses's sister, Miriam, who had been watching from a distance, stepped forward and volunteered to fetch Moses's mother to nurse this "unknown" baby. Pharaoh's daughter agreed.

Now Moses's mother got to experience a full-circle moment. I'm sure letting him go was the most painful thing she ever had to do, but in order to save him, she had to release him. There was a definite purpose for Moses's life, and because of that purpose, God protected him, put the right people in place, and, without a doubt, directed all of their paths. What are the odds that this child would be let go of, found, and brought back to the bosom of his very own mother? What are the odds that, having been drawn out of the water, Moses would deliver so many other children through a wall of water years later? It is certain that when God has a purpose for your life, it does not matter what the odds are. He places all the right pieces and people together to bring that purpose to fruition.

If you are a mother, teacher, nurse, mentor, social worker, or simply someone who loves people in general, God has strategically put you in place to help bring forth purpose in the lives of others. The kind words you give, the loving advice you offer, and even that strong word of correction are meaningful and purposeful in the development of someone's life. So never underestimate your influence in the lives of others. Never think that you're not needed or that what you have to say doesn't matter. It is all part of God's plan to help us all reach our purpose in life.

~~~~~~~~~~

POINTS TO PONDER

1. Do you know what your purpose in life is?

_____

_____

_____

2. Can you name a time when you knew your purpose was to help someone else complete their purpose? How did you help them?

_____

_____

_____

_____

3. Sometimes fear can hinder us from stepping forward to help others. Can you remember a time when you didn't step forward to help someone with their purpose? What was the hindrance? What _should_ you have done?

_____

_____

_____

_____

THIS IS MY PRAYER

Dear Lord,

It is my desire to please You in all of my ways. Help me always be a light and a positive role model in the lives of the people I encounter this week. I know that You have a purpose and plan for each of us. It is my prayer that You will help me daily *trust in You with all of my heart and lean not on my own understanding; but in all of my ways, I am trusting You to direct my path* (Proverbs 3:5–6, NKJV). Amen.

WEEK 4
THANK GOD FOR THE CRUSHING

DAILY READINGS

- Day 1: Exodus 19–21
- Day 2: Exodus 22–25
- Day 3: Exodus 26–29
- **Day 4: Exodus 30–32**
- Day 5: Exodus 33–36
- Day 6: Exodus 37–40
- Day 7: Catch up on any readings you've missed.

IN CHAPTERS 25 THROUGH 27 of Exodus, God instructed Moses how to set up the tabernacle (the holy tent used as a symbolic dwelling place for God before the first temple was built in Jerusalem). Chapters 28 and 29 tell us of the plans for the priests and their attire. God was very specific with His instructions. Before He would manifest His presence, everything in the tabernacle, including the priest, had to be anointed with specially prepared oil.

In Exodus 30, God gave Moses His very own recipe for this oil: 12½ pounds of pure myrrh, 6¼ pounds of cinnamon, 6¼ pounds of sweet calamus, 12½ pounds of cassia, and 1 gallon of olive oil (Exodus 30:22–24). Each ingredient chosen for the mixture had to be beaten, strained, or crushed. Of course, to obtain olive oil, you have to crush the olives—the more olives you crush, the more oil is produced.

You know, most of us have been crushed in some way. We've been crushed in relationships, at our jobs, in marriage, and even in ministry. But, unbeknownst to us, during those times of crushing, God was strategically anointing us for His service. The struggle that you experienced financially stretched you. The problems you endured with your spouse truly devastated you. The issues you encountered at your job put a strain on you. However, it was during those times that you found yourself leaning and depending on God in a way that you hadn't before. Those times forced you to increase your time of prayer, and you found yourself talking to God more and more each day. The crushing didn't feel good, but it was necessary to equip you and develop the anointing you needed to carry out your assignment on earth.

So when you feel the stress and strain of life, just know that it won't last forever and it is not in vain. Although the crushing is uncomfortable, God uses it to develop the oil needed to set us apart so that when others experience our ministries or gifts, it will be evident that God's hand is upon us. Don't despise the crushing—thank God for it!

POINTS TO PONDER

1. How have you been crushed or stretched in the last year? How did you handle it? Did you pray more or less? Did you go into hiding, or did you push to a better place?

   _____

   _____

   _____

2. Looking back now, how has God used that time of crushing for your good?

   _____

   _____

   _____

ACTIONS FOR THE WEEK

1. Make it a point to pray for someone who you know is going through a period of crushing. Pray especially for them this week that they will be able to endure the process.

2. Take action to bring that person solace by sending a note of encouragement, volunteering to babysit, or paying for lunch.

WEEK 5
I NEED WHAT
YOU HAVE

DAILY READINGS

Day 1: Matthew 1–3

Day 2: Matthew 4–7

Day 3: Matthew 8–11

Day 4: Matthew 12–15

Day 5: Matthew 16–19

Day 6: Matthew 20–22

Day 7: Catch up on any readings you've missed.

HAVE YOU EVER found yourself comparing your talents or gifts to someone else's? Have you ever felt like what you bring to the table doesn't compare to the abilities and assets of another? The truth is, we're not all meant to be the same or have the same level of ability. God uses our differences to let us complement and complete each other.

Matthew 3:13–17 tells of when Jesus and John met at the Jordan River, when Jesus was preparing to begin his ministry on earth. His cousin, John the Baptist, was well known in the area for uncompromisingly preaching the need for repentance and the Word of God. By divine inspiration from the Word of the prophets, John understood that someone was coming who would be greater than he could ever be. John baptized with water, but the One who was to come would baptize with the Holy Spirit.

One day, Jesus came to the Jordan to be baptized by John, but John strongly objected to the notion. Though he would gladly and boldly prepare the way for the One who was to come, John did not feel himself worthy to even fasten His shoes. But Jesus let John know that they were both needed in order to carry out God's divine purpose. Scripture says that Jesus never baptized anyone during His time of ministry on earth (John 4:1–2). By the same token, John the Baptist never performed any miracles (John 10:41). However, God needed *both* their ministries to carry out His plan.

You need to know that what you bring to the table is important and needed. You may not have the gifts that someone else has. You may not be able to sing, play an instrument, or write beautiful poetic words. But what you do is important, whether it's the kindness that you show to others or your ability to teach children. Not everybody is equipped to do all the things you do. You bring a little, and I'll bring the rest . . . or I'll bring a little, and you bring the rest. Either way, we need each other. So please don't underestimate your value and purpose. No matter your personal skill set or talents, someone needs what you have.

POINTS TO PONDER

1. What gifts do you bring to the table?

   _____

   _____

2. What are your strengths? What do you do well?

   _____

   _____

3. What has hindered you from using your gift?

   _____

   _____

ACTIONS FOR THE WEEK

1. Take a few minutes during your devotion time this week and pray for guidance about ways you can use the gifts you've been silently holding on to.

2. Think of ways you can help someone in an area where you now have confidence but once doubted yourself.

3. Think of ways you can help someone complete a task or project. You just may have what they need to complete their assignment and vice versa.

WEEK 6
TEAR DOWN
YOUR BARRIERS

DAILY READINGS

Day 1: Matthew 23–25

Day 2: Matthew 26–28

Day 3: Leviticus 1–4

Day 4: Leviticus 5–8

Day 5: Leviticus 9–12

Day 6: Leviticus 13–15

Day 7: Catch up on any readings you've missed.

RULES! RULES! RULES! Hardly anybody likes them, but everyone has to follow them. I've got rules. You've got rules. All of God's children should have rules and principles they live by according to their faith. An organization has policies and procedures. A church has a constitution and bylaws. Everybody has boundaries that others must comply with or be subject to the repercussions.

In the book of Leviticus, after the children of Israel had been released from Pharaoh, God gave Moses a set of rules on how to make atonement when they sinned. He didn't banish them; He understood that they had a natural tendency to sin, and He still wanted to have a relationship with them. The rules of atonement covered the Israelites' sins so they could be redeemed and forgiven. There were instructions for rituals and sacrifices—some for the purpose of saying, "I'm sorry," some simply to say, "Thank you." Leviticus 4–5 discusses the procedures for sin offerings, with special instructions for those who sinned unintentionally. Leviticus 5:18 says, "Through this process the priest will purify you from your unintentional sin, making you right with the Lord, and you will be forgiven."

How many times have we wanted to cut people off because they hurt us? How many times have we vowed never to speak to someone again because they betrayed our trust? How many times have we declared that we would rather give up on a certain individual because they simply refused to listen to our loving, opinionated, sometimes unsolicited, wise counsel? We can be so quick to push people away and banish them from our lives, but that's not the order or way of God. He not only gave the Israelites instructions for atonement, He also gave His only Son as a sacrifice for our wrongdoing, because He loves us unconditionally and He needed a way to redeem us from our sin. He didn't give up on us or see us as a lost cause. He showed His love toward us in spite of all of the wrongs we've done. The least we can do is return the favor by lovingly forgiving those who trespass against us. We can find a way to look past the flaws of others and maintain our covenant relationship.

These days, we need more covenant relationships. That may require you to tear down some of the barriers you've put up around your heart or make a few sacrifices of your own to obtain and maintain relationships with others. Don't be so quick to give up on people; God certainly did not give up on us. Before you make the decision to build more walls around your heart and life, think about how loving God was toward you. Let's do the same for others.

~~~~~~~~~~~~~~~~~~~~~~~~~~~~~~~~

POINTS TO PONDER

1. What are some of your rules for relationships with other people? What are your dos and don'ts?

_____

_____

_____

2. Do you have any deal breakers? Is there anything that will utterly destroy a friendship or relationship for you?

_____

_____

3. What grace have you given to others that you wish others would give to you?

_____

_____

_____

ACTIONS FOR THE WEEK

1. Make up your mind to show kindness to those who have not been so kind to you.

2. Make a list of those who may need your forgiveness—and try to forgive!

3. Ask yourself if there's anything that may be hindering your relationship with God. Make a list of those things, then take some time and pray the prayer of repentance, asking God to forgive you.

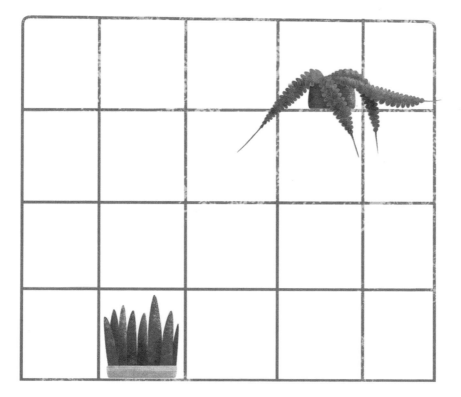

WEEK 7
PROSPER AND BE HAPPY

DAILY READINGS

Day 1: Psalms 1–3

Day 2: Leviticus 16–19

Day 3: Leviticus 20–23

Day 4: Psalms 4–6

Day 5: Leviticus 24–27

Day 6: Psalms 7–10

Day 7: Catch up on any readings you've missed.

I BELIEVE GOD'S purpose for us is to be all we can be, do all we're destined to do, and have all we're destined to have. I believe it's God's desire for us to do more than merely survive. In 3 John 1:2, John writes that he hopes his friend will prosper and be in good health as his soul prospers. God wants us to prosper. But what does it mean to prosper? It can mean to have economic success, to thrive, or to become strong and healthy. And I believe with all my heart, mind, and soul that this is God's will for our lives.

In Psalm 1, the psalmist lets us know that in order to position ourselves for the complete blessings of the Lord, there are certain things we must do or not do. The psalm begins with "Blessed is the one" (NIV)—in other words, happy is the one, or highly favored is the one, or prosperous is the one. Note that the psalmist didn't say blessed is the king, or blessed is the rich one, or blessed is the educated one. He said blessed is the *one*, which lets us know right away that the blessings are for us all. Your status doesn't matter. Your position doesn't matter. You *will* be blessed if you do your part.

What is your part? Verse 1 says you are blessed if you walk not in the counsel of the ungodly, nor stand in the pathway of sinners, nor sit in the seat of the scornful. Basically, if you want to be blessed, watch whom you're connected to, pay attention to your surroundings, and be careful of how you handle yourself while in those surroundings. Verse 2 says that we are blessed when our delight is in the law of the Lord and we willingly meditate on it day and night.

Verse 3 says that these behaviors will make you like a tree that is planted by rivers of water. Think about the analogy of the tree. There are some trees with roots that go straight down into the earth, and no matter how many storms come, no matter how hard the winds blow, those trees may bend—they may even lose a few leaves—but they're still rooted and grounded. And that's how we've got to be. We've got to stay rooted and grounded in our relationship with the Lord. As long as we do, we're bound to prosper and be blessed.

POINTS TO PONDER

1. How do you define prosperity?

_____

_____

_____

_____

2. Do you consider yourself prosperous? Why or why not?

_____

_____

_____

_____

3. What would be your advice to someone seeking to be prosperous?

_____

_____

_____

_____

THIS IS MY PRAYER

Dear Lord,

Help me find peace and prosperity in You alone. I pray that my days will be filled with joy and happiness so that I will have the capacity to share that joy and happiness with others. Make me like the tree that has been planted by rivers of water so that no matter what comes my way, I will continue to stand. Amen.

WEEK 8
THE BLESSING

DAILY READINGS

Day 1: Numbers 1–4

Day 2: Numbers 5–6

Day 3: Proverbs 1–3

Day 4: Numbers 7–9

Day 5: Numbers 10–13

Day 6: Proverbs 4–7

Day 7: Catch up on any readings you've missed.

I'VE BEEN A PART of the church all of my life, and one of the things I've known from childhood is that the benediction signifies the ending of the service. Of course, as a child, I didn't know the meaning of the word—I just knew that I wasn't supposed to leave before the benediction was pronounced by the pastor. But as we get older, we start to think we know it all, and we tend to get away from some of the principles we were brought up on. By the time I could drive myself to church, I'd come and go when I wanted. Sometimes I'd leave before the end of service, just because I could, or because I was headed to work and trying to beat the crowd out of the parking lot. As I became more familiar with the meaning of the benediction, however, I learned that it was God's blessing for His people, and I began to understand the need to remain in the service until the end, as it was a very special part of the worship.

This principle was established by God Himself and given as a directive to Moses for Aaron and his sons. In Numbers 6:23–26, God tells them specifically what to say when they pray and pronounce this blessing, starting with "The Lord bless you and keep you; the Lord make His face shine upon you" (NKJV). In other words, God's people need to know that God looks upon them and smiles because He is pleased with them. He is gracious toward them, showing them mercy and favor. He looks in their direction and gives them—us— peace. That is a gift and blessing in itself.

It was a long time before I understood how beautiful and meaningful this prayer of blessing would be in my life. This week, I encourage you to grab hold of this beautiful gift and apply it not only to your life but also to the lives of your children, spouse, family, and friends. When your children leave for school in the morning, pronounce the blessing. When your spouse leaves for work or a trip, pronounce the blessing. When your college-bound young adult leaves for the semester, pronounce the blessing. When a family gathering has come to an end and everyone prepares to leave, pronounce the blessing. You always want to make sure that everyone connected to you is just as blessed, safe, and at peace as you are.

POINTS TO PONDER

1. Did you know the meaning of the word "benediction"? What was/is your personal definition of the word?

_____

_____

2. Have you made a habit of audibly praying over your children, family, or friends? Why or why not?

_____

_____

3. I've named a few instances where the blessing of the Lord should be pronounced. Can you think of any others?

_____

_____

ACTIONS FOR THE WEEK

1. Make every effort to pronounce the blessing of the Lord over your children or other loved ones this week.

2. Begin to teach your children (or someone else who may not know) the meaning of this blessing and how necessary it is in our lives.

3. Make every effort to speak the blessing of the Lord over those you come into contact with this week.

WEEK 9
DELAY DOES NOT MEAN DENIAL

DAILY READINGS

Day 1: Numbers 14–16

Day 2: Numbers 17–19

Day 3: Numbers 20–22

Day 4: Proverbs 8–11

Day 5: Numbers 23–26

Day 6: Proverbs 12–14

Day 7: Catch up on any readings you've missed.

LAST YEAR, I WAS on a plane from Texas to North Carolina that was redirected to another destination midflight. We landed in South Carolina and sat in the middle of the tarmac for what seemed like hours. Many on board complained because they were missing their connecting flights. Many complained because they had been traveling all day and just wanted to get home. Eventually, I started to complain, too. As we waited, the pilot continued to say, "Thank you for your patience, we will be getting you to your destination very shortly." Each time we heard that statement, it sounded like nothing but an empty promise.

What we didn't know was that the pilot was avoiding flying us through a storm. We didn't know that because he'd been steering clear of the storm, we had been in the air so long that the plane needed to be refueled to complete its journey. We were doing all that complaining, not knowing that the pilot was taking the necessary measures to keep us safe.

That reminds me of a story in Numbers 14, when the children of Israel were delayed access to their Promised Land. In this chapter the children of Israel are instructed to get off their present course of travel, turn around, and take the long route through the wilderness—a journey that would last 40 years. God told them they couldn't go the short way because there were enemies waiting for them that they weren't prepared to fight. He made them go the long way through the wilderness.

But the wilderness was purposeful. It disciplined them, trained them, and prepared them to live as Promised Land people. In the wilderness, the naysayers died, and a new generation of believers was birthed. It did not take 40 years for God to get the children of Israel out of Egypt; it took 40 years to get Egypt out of the children of Israel. God delayed their arrival, but He did not deny them entrance into their Promised Land.

Many of us have questioned God and even complained because we felt like we were delayed and thrown off course. Many of us have felt like we should be further along than we are. Let me encourage

you, as I encourage myself, to hang in there just a little while longer. I know things may not be going the way you want them to go, but just know that you *will* walk into your promise. If you're like me on that plane, you might get frustrated because it feels like you're just waiting around for no reason, but you have to know that while you may have been delayed, you have not been denied.

POINTS TO PONDER

1. What area of your life do you feel is being delayed, and why do you feel that way?

   _____

   _____

   _____

2. How have you handled the delay?

_____

_____

_____

_____

3. After reading Numbers 14, do you identify with Joshua and Caleb, or do you think you would have been in agreement with the 10 who came back? Why?

_____

_____

_____

_____

THIS IS MY PRAYER

Dear Lord,
Help me submit to the process of delay. Help me wait patiently and trust that Your plans for me are definitely for good and not for evil. Father, I pray for wisdom while on this journey. Help me not look right or left but keep my focus on You, the author and finisher of my faith. Amen.

I'M JUST A VESSEL

DAILY READINGS

Day 1: Numbers 27–30

Day 2: Numbers 31–33

Day 3: Numbers 34–36

Day 4: Mark 1–5

Day 5: Mark 6–10

Day 6: Mark 11–16

Day 7: Catch up on any readings you've missed.

FOR MOST OF OUR LIVES, we've been told that women are the "weaker vessel" (1 Peter 3:7, KJV). Some will take this negatively, but the word "vessel" simply means "body." All that means is that the woman has the weaker body. And in most cases, we do. Being called a weaker vessel doesn't bother me, because that term has nothing to do with my intellect or my strength of spirit. It has nothing to do with what I'm able to accomplish in the marketplace, as an administrator, or as a teacher. I may be weaker in body, but I'm strong in so many other ways. A vessel is a receptacle or container, something that holds something else or pours its contents into other vessels. A vessel is designed to give to the point of emptying itself. Ladies, we have been designed to change the flow of everything around us simply because of what comes out of us. We might be the weaker vessel, but we also have the ability to provoke change in those around us.

This reminds me of a story in Numbers 27 about some sisters who proved their inner strength. The Bible says that after the death of their father, Zelophehad, these young women went to Moses and the other priests to plead for their father's portion of the inheritance. They argued that their father's name shouldn't have to be wiped out of the lineage just because he had all daughters and no sons. These sisters didn't settle. They didn't just go along with tradition. They pushed for change.

And Numbers 27:7–10 tells us that the girls won their case. The Lord said to Moses, "The daughters of Zelophehad speak what is right; you shall surely give them a possession of inheritance among their father's brothers, and cause the inheritance of their father to pass to them" (NKJV). The sisters' boldness paid off not just for them but also for the girls who would come after them. They were women, but they were trailblazers who changed the rules for all women to come.

Unfortunately, there are a lot of people who just see the exterior. They just see the woman. Many can't look past the vessel to see the power of what it can do. We might be women, but we are women who blaze trails. We strive to make a difference. You're not helpless; you're not hopeless. You are a strong and powerful overcomer, and you deserve everything God has in store for you. So tap into your girl power and be who God created you to be.

POINTS TO PONDER

1. In what ways have you underestimated yourself?

_____

_____

2. In what ways do you believe others have underestimated you, perhaps because you're a woman?

_____

_____

3. If you could change a rule to benefit others, what would it be?

_____

_____

THIS IS MY PRAYER

Dear Lord,
Help me be the vessel You created me to be. I cast out all fears, because You have not given me a spirit of fear but one of love, power, and a sound mind. Help me make an impact on those I encounter. It is my desire to please You as well as make a difference on the earth. Amen.

WEEK 11
BEARING
BURDENS

DAILY READINGS

Day 1: Deuteronomy 1–4

Day 2: Deuteronomy 5–8

Day 3: Psalms 11–14

Day 4: Deuteronomy 9–11

Day 5: Deuteronomy 12–15

Day 6: Psalms 15–17

Day 7: Catch up on any readings you've missed.

TRANSITION CAN BE A MEANS of evolving into something better, but you must be sure that you're intentional in how you do it, because the enemy always seems to turn up the heat when you're going through transition. It's when you find out how strong you are and how strong your prayer life is. In Deuteronomy 1, we find Moses addressing the children of Israel, reminding them of their journey. He goes over all the twists and turns of their trek through the wilderness to help them understand where they've come from and where they're going. I submit that at this point, Moses isn't just trying to help *them* understand—he's trying to make sense of his *own* process of transition, too.

He starts off by reminding them of when the Lord told them they'd been stuck for too long at Mount Horeb and it was time to move on. God told them which path they'd have to travel and that they'd occupy the same land their ancestors were promised. Then Moses has an honest moment. He remembers how the children of Israel have grown into a much larger multitude than when they started out and admits he can't handle their many issues on his own: "How can I bear your problems and your burdens and your disputes all by myself?" (Deuteronomy 1:12, NIV). Therefore, he follows the Lord's directive and appoints "wise, understanding and respected men" (Deuteronomy 1:13, NIV) from within the community to help carry the load of the people.

Moses sees this need more than ever while in transition, because when people are shifting from one place to the next, it can be challenging, confusing, and chaotic. When you're a leader or someone others rely on, sometimes your community's challenges become your challenges, and their confusion becomes your confusion. You're handling their problems. You're finding solutions for them. But are you also relieving them of responsibility or accountability?

In a season of transition from better to best, you've got to let everybody work out their own salvation. Yes, we are called to strengthen our brothers and sisters, and we've been directed to help them bear their burdens when they are weak. But we're not designed to carry all of the load ourselves—not even Moses was. Galatians 6:5 says that each one shall bear his own load. You may be accustomed to bailing everybody out, and of course you want to help as much as you can. But we shouldn't enable people or prevent them from growing. Instead, encourage, empower, and celebrate them—but hold them accountable to carry their own load in the midst of their transition.

POINTS TO PONDER

1. Would you consider yourself an enabler or one who empowers? Why?

_____

_____

_____

_____

2. As moms, leaders, or sisters, we have a tendency to run to the rescue. Can you think of a time when you intervened when you should have allowed someone to figure something out for themselves? What were the results?

_____

_____

_____

_____

3. Can you see yourself transitioning from one level to the next right now? How has your process been?

_____

_____

_____

_____

ACTIONS FOR THE WEEK

1. Write a list of people you're "supposed to" help and how you think you're supposed to help them. Make note of exactly how much you'll help and where you'll draw the line.

2. If you believe you're going through a transition, big or small, list the steps you can take to be successful. Make a timeline to help you meet your goals.

WEEK 12
BLESSED OR CURSED

DAILY READINGS

- Day 1: Deuteronomy 16–18
- Day 2: Deuteronomy 19–21
- Day 3: Psalms 18–21
- Day 4: Deuteronomy 22–25
- **Day 5: Deuteronomy 26–28**
- Day 6: Psalms 22–25
- Day 7: Catch up on any readings you've missed.

IN DEUTERONOMY 28, we find Moses presenting the nation of Israel with two options. The God who made a covenant with the children of Israel gives them a choice to be blessed or cursed. If given that choice, quite naturally we'd choose to be blessed, because we all want to be blessed. But you have to ask yourself: Have you positioned yourself to be blessed?

The Word of the Lord came to Moses to tell the children of Israel that *if* they listened diligently to the voice of the Lord and were watchful to do all His commandments, *then* all of these blessings would come upon them. Many of us listen to the Word week after week, but how much of it do we really hold on to or apply to our lives? How much of it do we take as the living Word of God?

I don't know about you, but I'm at a place in my life where I can't afford to take any more detours. I can't afford to waste time or make any more mistakes. I need to know the exact direction that I am to go in. If things are going to work together for my good, I've got to be in His will. If you're like me, you need real direction. If you're like me, you don't like confusion; you need clarity about where to go and what to do. Well, in order to position yourself for the blessings of God, you've got to learn how to recognize the voice of God and listen to what He says.

And not only are we to listen to what God says—we also need to do what He says. You see, it's one thing to listen, but it's a whole other thing to do what we're told. And sometimes that's where we mess up. We don't mind listening. In fact, we show up faithfully every week to listen, but we miss the mark when it comes to doing. That's where obedience comes into play.

Have you done what God told you to do? The ball is in your court. You have a choice. Do you want to be blessed?

~~~~~~~~~~~~~~~~~~~~~~~~~~~~~~~~~~~~~~

POINTS TO PONDER

1. Have you positioned yourself to be blessed? Are you listening and doing? Has that been difficult to do? Why?

    _____

    _____

    _____

    _____

2. Have you ever felt like you were more cursed than blessed? How did you reverse the curse?

    _____

    _____

    _____

    _____

ACTIONS FOR THE WEEK

1. Make a list of your blessings, and make it a point to thank God for each one of them every day this week.

2. Make a list of the commands that you have failed to fulfill, whether it be helping, forgiving, or giving to someone. Begin to cross them off your list one by one this week.

YOUR OWN JORDAN RIVER

DAILY READINGS

- Day 1: Deuteronomy 29–31
- Day 2: Deuteronomy 32–34
- **Day 3: Joshua 1–4**
- Day 4: Joshua 5–8
- Day 5: Joshua 9–12
- Day 6: Joshua 13–16
- Day 7: Catch up on any readings you've missed.

JOSHUA 3 TELLS THE STORY of how Joshua and the children of Israel crossed the Jordan River. These were the people who had been delivered from the hands of Pharaoh and out of Egypt. They had crossed the Red Sea. Then, after 40 years in the wilderness, they came upon one last stumbling block between them and their Promised Land: the Jordan River. They were facing 200 miles of pure discouragement. Why? At that time of the year, the Jordan River was swollen and overflowing because of the rains during the harvest season. The Israelites camped out on the banks of the Jordan for three days, presumably trying to figure out how to cross it. They were stuck.

Maybe you're not where you used to be, but you're stuck in a place you're not destined to be—your own Jordan River. Your Jordan could be financial, mental, emotional, or even spiritual. Whatever the case may be, you have found yourself in a place where you wish you were not. You're in good company, however, because we've all been there at some point in our lives. We are anointed, we have gifts and talents, but we've all been stuck. We're just not meant to stay there.

Joshua sought directions from the Lord about how to cross the river, and he received them. God instructed Joshua to have the priests, who were transporting the Ark of the Covenant, "take a few steps into the river and stop there . . . As soon as their feet touch the water, the flow of water will be cut off upstream, and the river will stand up like a wall" (Joshua 3:8–13). That's exactly what they did, and "they waited there until the whole nation of Israel had crossed the Jordan on dry ground" (Joshua 3:17).

Whatever season we're in, we need God's clear instructions to face our own rivers. We've got to be like Joshua and the children of Israel, seeking the face of the Lord for strategy and direction. If God says to move, then we must move. If He says to speak, then we have to muster the boldness to speak His heart. If He says to be still, then we must do so until His will is clear. If we're to cross our Jordan, obedience to the voice of the Lord must be our top priority.

I don't know about you, but I refuse to stay stuck and settle for less than what I'm destined to receive and achieve.

POINTS TO PONDER

1. In what areas of your life have you ever felt stuck?

_____

_____

2. How did you handle things? Did you seek guidance or wise counsel?

_____

_____

3. How did you begin to make moves again? What did you do to get out of the rut you were in?

_____

_____

VERSE OF THE WEEK

Be strong and very courageous. Be careful to obey all the instructions Moses gave you. Do not deviate from them, turning either to the right or to the left. Then you will be successful in everything you do. Study this Book of Instruction continually. Meditate on it day and night so you will be sure to obey everything written in it. Only then will you prosper and succeed in all you do. This is my command—be strong and courageous! Do not be afraid or discouraged. For the Lord your God is with you wherever you go.
▶ **Joshua 1:7–9**

WEEK 14
I AM
A WINNER!

DAILY READINGS

☐ Day 1: Joshua 17–20

☐ Day 2: Joshua 21–24

☐ Day 3: Proverbs 15–17

☐ Day 4: Judges 1–3

☐ Day 5: Judges 4–6

☐ **Day 6: Judges 7–10**

☐ Day 7: Catch up on any readings you've missed.

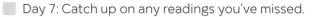

AROUND THIS COUNTRY, football, basketball, and baseball seasons are as defining as winter, spring, summer, and fall. We live in a competitive society. We love to see a team working together to win the game. Well, whether we know it or not, we're all in a game. That game is life, and we have an adversary who does not want to see us win, to see our families flourish, or to see our marriages work. He doesn't want our businesses to be successful or us to be happy and complete. There's a lot on the line, and there will be a winner and a loser. I don't know about you, but I've made up my mind that I'm going to win this one.

In the book of Judges, we find an account of how God gave Gideon victory over his enemy. In Judges 6, Israel had become rebellious, and God allowed the nation of Midian to take dominion over them. But then God had mercy and assigned Gideon to go and rescue them. Gideon didn't think he had what it took to accomplish the assignment. His tribe was the weakest of the bunch, and there was no way they'd be able to take the Midianites. So Gideon asked God for a sign, and God gave it to him. In fact, God gave him several signs to prove that He was with him, because Gideon was like a lot of us; we don't always take God at His word, and we want sign after sign so that we can be assured He's going to do what He said.

When Gideon was finally convinced, he brought an army of 32,000 men to battle the Midianites. But God had him send home all but 300, saying He would provide victory (Judges 7:7). God kept his promise. With just 300 men, Gideon was victorious over the Midianites.

Sometimes, you just have to stand on what God says alone. That's what faith is. According to Hebrews 11:1, "faith is the substance of things hoped for, the evidence of things not seen" (KJV). When you don't have the evidence, you have to trust what He says, even if it doesn't make sense. If God has already called you a winner, you are a winner. If God has said you are a success, then you are a success. You don't need a sign or a secret code; you just need to remember what He said. In spite of the odds, we have to always remember that if God is for us, He is more than the whole world against us (Romans 8:31). That kind of favor swings the odds our way and makes us winners!

~~~~~~~~~~~~~~~~~~~~~~~~

POINTS TO PONDER

1. Would you have trusted God's instructions to send most of your men home? Why or why not?

_____

_____

2. Has there been a time in your life when you trusted God and succeeded against the odds?

_____

_____

3. In Judges 7:9–11, God instructs Gideon to go to his enemy's camp. Why, and what were the results?

_____

_____

VERSE OF THE WEEK

The Lord told Gideon, "With these 300 men I will rescue you and give you victory over the Midianites. Send all the others home." So Gideon collected the provisions and rams' horns of the other warriors and sent them home. But he kept the 300 men with him.

The Midianite camp was in the valley just below Gideon. That night the Lord said, "Get up! Go down into the Midianite camp, for I have given you victory over them!" ▶Judges 7:7–9

WEEK 15
TRUST HIS
TRACK RECORD

DAILY READINGS

Day 1: Judges 11–14

Day 2: Judges 15–17

Day 3: Judges 18–21

Day 4: Psalms 26–29

Day 5: Psalms 30–33

Day 6: Psalms 34–37

Day 7: Catch up on any readings you've missed.

IN PSALM 30, we find David reminiscing, thanking God for His sovereignty, and reflecting on the Lord's goodness toward him. He remembers a time when he didn't always do the right thing, but God was merciful. When he began to really prosper, David got a little full of himself and started doing things his own way. When he began to operate in error, he felt that God had hidden His face from him—but that didn't last long. David says in verse 5, "For His anger is but for a moment, His favor is for life; weeping may endure for a night, but joy comes in the morning" (NKJV). You see, even though he did wrong, David remembered God's grace toward him.

Let me encourage you to take a moment and reflect on God's grace and mercy to you. When we think of how kind and gracious God has been to us, in spite of ourselves, it should give us a true heart of gratitude. All it takes is a memory of a moment of grace. Then you can get excited about what He's going to do, because whatever God has done before, He is God enough to do again. While you're in the midst of your struggle, it's hard to fathom how things will turn out, but if you've been restored before, you can be again. If He favored you with a great job opportunity before, He can do so again. There is no limit when it comes to God. He didn't promise to bless you one time and that was it. He didn't promise to heal you only once and that would be the end of your healing. He didn't promise to open only one door for you and that's the end of the story.

Jesus died so that we'd all be saved, and that should give us assurance that He's not finished yet, because there are souls yet to be saved. We have seen how He has covered us through massive storms, kept us through terrible car wrecks, and spared the lives of family members. I believe He can be trusted to do those things again and so much more. There is no limit to what our God can do!

If we can just hold on to what God has already done, we will immediately begin to get excited about the possibilities of our future. Just as David stated, "His anger is but for a moment, His favor is for life." I don't know about anyone else, but I am thankful that even though I make mistakes, God looks beyond them and extends His favor. That gives me hope for my future and the blessings that are sure to come. So I admonish you to trust God's track record. Trust that whatever blessings of the Lord you once received can be brought to your life again. Trust His track record.

POINTS TO PONDER

1. Can you remember a time when God was gracious although you felt you didn't deserve His kindness?

   _____

   _____

2. How has God's compassion toward you taught you to be compassionate toward others?

   _____

   _____

3. Sometimes trust can be a hard thing. What hard thing in your life will you trust God to do?

   _____

   _____

ACTIONS FOR THE WEEK

1. Take some time to remember and list how God has blessed you.

2. Starting next week, take some time each day to give thanks for your blessings.

STOP STRESSING AND START PRAYING

DAILY READINGS

Day 1: Ruth 1–4

Day 2: 1 Samuel 1–3

Day 3: 1 Samuel 4–7

Day 4: 1 Samuel 8–11

Day 5: 1 Samuel 12–14

Day 6: 1 Samuel 15–17

Day 7: Catch up on any readings you've missed.

IN 1 SAMUEL 1, we find the story of a woman who experienced a void in her life. Her name was Hannah, and she was childless because the Lord had closed her womb (1 Samuel 1:6, NKJV). To make matters worse, her husband's other wife, Peninnah, did have children. Keep in mind that children were a sign of worth and a basis for security, so the mere fact that the Lord had not allowed Hannah to have children left her feeling worthless, incomplete, and hopeless. At the time, she didn't know what God had in store for her. She could only see what she didn't have and couldn't do, and this put her in a bad mental and emotional place.

Hannah felt so much stress that she couldn't eat. Her husband, Elkanah, tried to make her feel better by giving her a double portion of his possessions, but that wasn't what she wanted or needed. So what did she do? She didn't complain, blame her husband, or start a fight with Peninnah out of jealousy. She went to the temple and began to pour out her soul to God.

The problem with many of us is that we tend to pour out our souls to other people, hoping they'll give us answers, when most times they can only offer us their opinions. We have to take our struggles to the One who has the power to answer our prayers and solve our problems. That's what Hannah did. She went to the temple and prayed so intently that Eli, the priest, thought she was drunk and asked her when she'd be ready to quit drinking. She responded, "No, my lord, I am a woman of sorrowful spirit. I have drunk neither wine nor intoxicating drink, but have poured out my soul before the Lord" (1 Samuel 1:15, NKJV). That's when Eli told her to go in peace and that God would grant her what she'd asked for.

After that, Hannah went on her way and was no longer sad. Of course, if you've read to the end of the story, you know that Hannah was ultimately responsible for birthing Samuel, one of the greatest prophets recorded in scripture. But even before she conceived, it gave Hannah peace to be able to pour out her soul to the Lord and speak her truth to Eli.

Many of us hold on to things we can't change. We internalize them and allow them to stress us out to the point of anxiety and depression. I encourage you to free yourself from those things by pouring out your soul to the Lord. Have an honest moment with yourself, admit what has you troubled, and then trust God enough to give it to Him to handle. While you're waiting on God to help you, He may be waiting on you to cry out to Him.

POINTS TO PONDER

1. What is at the top of your stress list? Why is it such a stressor?

   _____

   _____

   _____

2. How do you normally handle those things that you have no control over? (Be honest!)

   _____

   _____

   _____

   _____

3. After reading Hannah's story, what have you learned about yourself? Going forward, how will you handle your stress?

   _____

   _____

   _____

   _____

VERSE OF THE WEEK

The entire family got up early the next morning and went to worship the Lord once more. Then they returned home to Ramah. When Elkanah slept with Hannah, the Lord remembered her plea, and in due time she gave birth to a son. She named him Samuel, for she said, "I asked the Lord for him." ▶ 1 Samuel 1:19–20

WEEK 17
MOVING THE ARK

DAILY READINGS

Day 1: 1 Samuel 18–21

Day 2: 1 Samuel 22–25

Day 3: 1 Samuel 26–29

Day 4: 1 Samuel 30–31

Day 5: 2 Samuel 1–4

Day 6: 2 Samuel 5–8

Day 7: Catch up on any readings you've missed.

IN 2 SAMUEL 5, the Philistines hear about David being anointed as king over Israel, and they set out to find him and destroy him. David learns of the impending attack and goes to the Lord for direction. He waits and listens for God's instructions and is victorious when he follows them exactly. As a leader, David is certain that listening to God should always come before action.

In 2 Samuel 6, after defeating the Philistines in battle twice, David is faced with another leadership challenge. He's preparing to bring the Ark of the Lord back to its rightful place in Jerusalem after it was briefly captured by the Philistines. The Ark is a holy, gold-plated chest carrying the tablets of the Ten Commandments, and it has to be handled according to very specific rules. But this time, David doesn't ask God for instructions. Instead, he and his men retrieve the Ark from the house of Abinadab and assign Abinadab's sons, Uzzah and Ahio, to transport it to Jerusalem. David and all the people of Israel are singing and celebrating alongside the cart—but then the oxen stumble. Uzzah reaches out to steady the Ark, and God immediately strikes him dead.

What went wrong? The people involved did things the way *they* thought was best instead of listening to God. The Lord had laid out rules for transporting the Ark, and they did not include putting it on a cart. It may have been convenient for David and his men to move the Ark this way, but it wasn't how God told them to do it. What God *did* tell them was that no one could touch the Ark (see Numbers 4:15). When Uzzah reached out to keep the Ark from falling, he made a split-second decision that he thought was right, but it cost him his life.

Both these passages clearly illustrate why it behooves us to pray before we act. Proverbs 3:5–6 says, "Trust in the Lord with all your heart, and lean not on your own understanding; in all your ways acknowledge Him, and He shall direct your paths" (NKJV). When we trust God, we're victorious, as David was over the Philistines. Unfortunately, sometimes we overlook some of the directions we've received. We begin to do things out of convenience instead of how we've been instructed.

This is a classic example of how our obedience to God affects everybody around us, including our families, our coworkers, and our fellow laborers in ministry. We should make sure we're hearing from God and following His directions, not based on what we feel or think but on what He said. And when it seems like God is not speaking, you've got to recall what He has already said. It has to be His way, because His way is always right!

POINTS TO PONDER

1. Have you ever made a move that you probably should have prayed about first? Were there repercussions?

_____

_____

_____

_____

2. Why do we sometimes find it easier to go our own way than to seek direction from God?

_____

_____

_____

_____

3. Going forward, how will you handle your decisions, great and small?

_____

_____

_____

_____

THIS IS MY PRAYER

Dear Lord,
Help me seek You in all that I do. It is my desire to be in Your divine and perfect will—not just for me, but for all those who are connected to me. I vow today to seek Your face, listen for Your voice, and be led by Your mighty hand. In Jesus's name, amen.

WEEK 18
GOD HAS NOT FORGOTTEN

DAILY READINGS

Day 1: 2 Samuel 9–12

Day 2: 2 Samuel 13–15

Day 3: 2 Samuel 16–18

Day 4: 2 Samuel 19–21

Day 5: 2 Samuel 22–24

Day 6: Psalms 38–41

Day 7: Catch up on any readings you've missed.

IN 2 SAMUEL 9, we see how David finds a way to show kindness to Mephibosheth—the son of his best friend, Jonathan, and the grandson of his worst enemy, Saul. When the nurse caring for five-year-old Mephibosheth heard that Saul and Jonathan had died in battle, she grabbed the child and ran. In her haste, she dropped him, and both of his feet were broken, disabling him permanently. Back then, if you were disabled, you would have a hard time earning a living (even harder than today), and many people wouldn't be able to see past your differences to appreciate your worth. Because this happened to him as a child, Mephibosheth spent most of his life not being able to recognize his own value. When we see him in 2 Samuel 9, he's a grown man, living in someone else's house in a small town called Lo-Debar, unable to provide for himself.

In 1 Samuel 20:14–15, Jonathan says, "And may you treat me with the faithful love of the Lord as long as I live. But if I die, treat my family with this faithful love, even when the Lord destroys all your enemies from the face of the earth." Years later, David has not forgotten the promise he made. When David engages with Mephibosheth, he says to him, "Don't be afraid . . . I intend to show kindness to you because of my promise to your father, Jonathan. I will give you all the property that once belonged to your grandfather Saul, and you will eat here with me at the king's table!" (2 Samuel 9:7).

Mephibosheth has always felt like nothing. In fact, in verse 8, he asks David, "Who is your servant, that you should show such kindness to a dead dog like me?" He very possibly wants to be forgotten because of the wicked things his grandfather, Saul, did. But David wants to bless him because of the promise he made to his father, Jonathan. Mephibosheth can't fathom anyone showing him this type of favor, but God has plans beyond his comprehension.

God has not forgotten about you, either. It has nothing to do with you or anything that you've done, right or wrong. It's all because of God's favor. Even if it seems against the odds, there is still favor over your life. The blessings that God has for you are coming in spite of you, not because of you. The truth is, we're all flawed. But God looks past those flaws and still supplies our needs. He even gives us some of our wants. God still has you on His mind. Like Mephibosheth, you may not feel favored, but you are highly favored. You may not feel blessed, but you are better than blessed.

POINTS TO PONDER

1. Has there ever been a time in your life when you couldn't see your own value? What were the circumstances surrounding that season of your life?

2. How did you get released from that kind of thinking? Do you struggle with it still?

3. How would you encourage someone else who may find it hard to realize their value?

ACTIONS FOR THE WEEK

1. Brainstorm ways to show kindness to someone this week.

2. Think of a kindness that has been shown to you at some point. Then be intentional and pay it forward to someone else.

3. Find a way to put a smile on the face of someone who you know has been low in spirit.

4. Send someone a message and remind them that God has not forgotten about them.

THE DROUGHT IS ALMOST OVER

DAILY READINGS

Day 1: 1 Kings 1–4

Day 2: 1 Kings 5–7

Day 3: 1 Kings 8–10

Day 4: 1 Kings 11–14

Day 5: 1 Kings 15–18

Day 6: 1 Kings 19–22

Day 7: Catch up on any readings you've missed.

HAVE YOU EVER NOTICED how the atmosphere feels when there's a storm on the horizon? The wind begins to blow, but it's still warm outside. Soon, the clouds cover the sun, and the wind shifts and becomes a little stronger. To someone inexperienced, these changes may not seem significant. But if you've lived for a while, you can tell a storm is about to arrive, because you've seen these changes before.

We see this kind of feeling in the atmosphere around the prophet Elijah in 1 Kings 18—figuratively and literally. Elijah had prophesied that no rain would fall for three years to prove to the wicked King Ahab and other idol worshipers that Yahweh (a biblical name for God, often anglicized as Jehovah) was the true and living God, not Baal or any of the other false gods being worshiped. In this passage, those three years were complete, and Elijah and Ahab were in a confrontation. In a competition against the prophets of Baal at Mount Carmel, God allowed Elijah to perform miracles and call down fire from heaven. We see Elijah succeed in killing all the prophets of Baal. And then Elijah says to King Ahab, *Go and get you something good to eat, because I hear the rain coming.*

Rain after three years of drought would be the miracle that confirmed who the true God was. Elijah was certain about this. It wasn't about what he felt. It was about what he *heard.* We have to always guard our ears, because it is through the ear that we hear the Word of the Lord for our lives. Romans 10:17 says, "So then faith comes by hearing, and hearing by the word of God" (NKJV). And in 1 Kings, what Elijah heard was an abundance of rain.

Then Ahab went to get something to eat and to drink, but Elijah went to pray. I believe that he prayed for God to manifest what he heard so strongly in his spirit. And that's a lesson for us all. Sometimes God will drop something in your spirit that doesn't seem possible, but you sense it so strongly. You can't explain it, but you just know that something is on the horizon. Therefore, we must pray for God to manifest what He's already spoken in our spirits. You might not know when or how it's coming to pass, but I encourage you to continue in prayer, trusting that the drought is almost over and God is soon to bring forth manifestation.

POINTS TO PONDER

1. What areas of your life are seemingly in a season of drought?

_____

_____

_____

_____

2. What impossible thing have you been sensing in your spirit?

_____

_____

_____

_____

3. Why is it so impossible? Do you really believe that God can and will perform the work?

_____

_____

_____

_____

FURTHER THOUGHTS FOR THE WEEK

After Elijah prays, he tells his servant to go look toward the sea. The servant comes back and says he didn't see anything. Elijah keeps sending him back until, on the seventh time, his servant sees a little cloud about the size of a man's hand rising from the sea. Elijah is persistent in his faith. He doesn't allow one, two, or six bad reports to discourage him. He stands on what God said, and he doesn't waver. We won't always see immediate manifestation, but that doesn't mean God isn't going to do what He said. We must be persistent in our faith, knowing that if God said it, it's got to come to pass.

WEEK 20
BOUNCING
BACK

DAILY READINGS

Day 1: 2 Kings 1–3

Day 2: 2 Kings 4–7

Day 3: 2 Kings 8–11

Day 4: 2 Kings 12–15

Day 5: 2 Kings 16–18

Day 6: 2 Kings 19–22

Day 7: Catch up on any readings you've missed.

WOMEN OF GOD, I'm sure you have much to be thankful for. You have many testimonies of God's grace and how He's kept you and provided for you. By the same token, I'm sure there have been days when you were disappointed and frustrated, times when you just weren't sure what tomorrow would bring. But God sustained you and even gave you the power to get back up. I'm a living witness of that kind of experience, and I thank God for the ability to bounce back. Is it always easy? Absolutely not! But it is doable with God's help.

In 2 Kings 8, we find the story of a woman who literally had to walk away from everything she owned. This woman had been a faithful servant to the prophet Elisha; in chapter 4, she and her husband built a room onto their home so the prophet would have a place to stay whenever he was in town. Elisha, wanting to repay her, spoke a word over her life, and she and her husband were blessed against all odds with a son. Later, the same son they were blessed with died. But this woman's faith never waned. She went to the prophet to beg for her son's life, and it was miraculously restored.

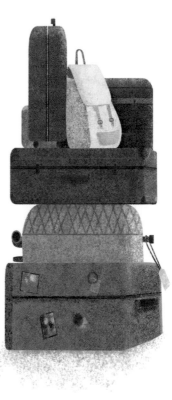

Now, in chapter 8, she was getting ready to go through yet another crisis, and the one constant thing she still had going for her was that her faith was strong. Elisha told her to leave her home and find somewhere to live in another land, because the Lord was going to cause a seven-year famine. So here we have this woman who was once very wealthy. She had to go through a period when her child was sick unto death. She had evidently lost her husband, and now she was about to lose her home. Her faith was strong, but she was still going through her share of struggles. Yet, in spite of it all, we see her bouncing back strong. When she got back to town, she went to see the king to ask for the return of her land. She got back everything she had lost plus the profit the land had produced from the day she left until the day she returned.

Let me encourage you as I encourage myself. There will be some ups and downs in all our lives. Some days, we'll feel like we're on top of the world; other days, we'll wonder, *Where is God?* Do not fear, my dear sister; God is still right there. You may not know how or when, but He will give you the power to bounce back!

POINTS TO PONDER

1. Can you identify in any way with the story of the woman from 2 Kings? How?

_____

_____

_____

_____

2. Has there ever been a time when you've wondered where God was? How did you handle it?

_____

_____

_____

_____

3. After reading this story, can you see the importance of persevering in faith and obedience? How do you feel about your level of faith? Your obedience?

_____

_____

_____

_____

VERSE OF THE WEEK

And when the king asked the woman, she told him.

So the king appointed a certain officer for her, saying, "Restore all that was hers, and all the proceeds of the field from the day that she left the land until now." ▶ **2 Kings 8:6 (NKJV)**

WEEK 21
CAN YOU PASS THE TEST?

DAILY READINGS

- Day 1: 2 Kings 23–25
- **Day 2: Luke 1–4**
- Day 3: Luke 5–7
- Day 4: Luke 8–11
- Day 5: Luke 12–14
- Day 6: Luke 15–18
- Day 7: Catch up on any readings you've missed.

THE BIBLE TELLS OF JESUS being tested before He began His ministry on earth: "Jesus, full of the Holy Spirit, returned from the Jordan River. He was led by the Spirit in the wilderness, where he was tempted by the devil for forty days" (Luke 4:1-2). Notice that first line about returning from the Jordan full of the Spirit. Remember, He had just been baptized by John the Baptist. A dove descended upon Him, and God Himself spoke and said, "You are My beloved Son; in You I am well pleased" (Luke 3:22, NKJV). No sooner did Jesus get this confirmation from on high than He was sent to the wilderness and put to the test.

In the wilderness, Satan quoted scripture out of context to try to get Jesus to go against the will of God. He came at Jesus at a time when His spirit was strong but His body was weak. He was hungry, so Satan tried to appeal to His flesh. Satan does the same thing to us. He comes in times of blessing and of drought. He comes against the strong as well as the weak. He doesn't care if you're sick, overworked, or dealing with pressures at home. He will use every circumstance to work his plan.

The higher we go, the greater the test will be. You'll be tested in ways you've never been tested before. The test might come in your marriage, when your husband has been laid off from his job and you're solely responsible for the bills. The test might come in your body, when the doctor says you have cancer. But the good news is that we're not in this thing by ourselves.

One way to be assured of that is to make sure God's Word is within us. That's how Jesus passed His test. Each time Satan came at Jesus with a temptation, Jesus came back at him with the Word. He said, "It is written: 'Man shall not live by bread alone, but on every word that comes from the mouth of God'" (Matthew 4:4, NIV). The Word is our armor and our weapon, according to Ephesians 6:17. Hebrews 4:12 says the Word "is living and powerful, and sharper than any two-edged sword" (NKJV). Jesus used it to defeat Satan, and we have to be able to do the same. The Word of God is the greatest tool needed in order to pass our tests of life. If it worked for Jesus, it can work for us.

~~~

POINTS TO PONDER

1. What tests have you encountered lately?

_____

_____

_____

2. Did you pass or fail your test? How did you do it?

_____

_____

_____

3. What advice would you give someone going through a test?

_____

_____

_____

ACTIONS FOR THE WEEK

1. Knowing that the Word of God is your only weapon, commit yourself to learning and committing to memory a new verse each day this week.

2. For each verse that you learn, try to think of a way that verse can be applied to your daily activities and challenges.

WEEK 22
BE STILL

DAILY READINGS

■ Day 1: Luke 19–21

■ Day 2: Luke 22–24

■ **Day 3: Psalms 42–47**

■ Day 4: Psalms 48–54

■ Day 5: Psalms 55–61

■ Day 6: Psalms 62–67

■ Day 7: Catch up on any readings you've missed.

PSALM 46 IS A SONG for the descendants of Korah. It was a song that they sang as they encouraged each other to continue to trust God even in the midst of rough times. This psalm is meant to encourage us to have hope and trust in the all-powerful God and to remind us of who our God is.

In Psalm 46:1–9 (GNT), the psalmist says:

God is our shelter and strength, always ready to help in times of trouble. So we will not be afraid, even if the earth is shaken and mountains fall into the ocean depths . . . The Lord Almighty is with us; the God of Jacob is our refuge. Come and see what the Lord has done. See what amazing things he has done on earth. He stops wars all over the world; he breaks bows, destroys spears, and sets shields on fire.

In other words, the psalmist is saying: *Don't you know who our God is? He is a God who is able to do all things, and He controls everything!* And so, because God has everything under control, the psalmist says, "Be still, and know" (verse 10, NIV). Be still and know the kind of God you have on your side, fighting for you and watching over you. Just be still. Now, being still in this sense doesn't mean being inactive or complacent. It means waiting with assurance, knowing that God is working things out for your good. It means that, while you're waiting, you trust that God is behind the scenes working on your behalf.

Sometimes it's hard to be still and wait on God when you really need Him to move. It can be a hard thing to do when your family's finances are in trouble or your children are heading down a road of destruction. At those critical times, being still might not make sense to us. We likely want to handle the situation or find a solution to the problem. But when God is not moving or speaking, when He seems to be taking forever to work it out, that may be a sign for you to be still. I know it's hard, but sometimes God wants to build your faith and develop your testimony. Whatever the reason, we have to learn to trust His plan and simply be still.

~~~~~~~~~~~~~~~~~~~~~~~~~~~~~~~~~~~~~~

POINTS TO PONDER

1. How many times this week have you made moves when you should have been still? For example, did you argue with your husband when you should have held your peace? Speak up for your daughter instead of allowing her to learn to speak up for herself?

   ----

2. In what areas of your life do you find it most difficult to be still?

   ----

3. Going forward, how will you challenge yourself to be still and trust God?

VERSE OF THE WEEK

Be still, and know that I am God; I will be exalted among the nations, I will be exalted in the earth. ▸ **Psalm 46:10 (NIV)**

WEEK 23
HIS WAY IS THE RIGHT WAY

DAILY READINGS

Day 1: 1 Chronicles 1–4

Day 2: 1 Chronicles 5–8

Day 3: 1 Chronicles 9–12

Day 4: 1 Chronicles 13–16

Day 5: 1 Chronicles 17–19

Day 6: 1 Chronicles 20–22

Day 7: Catch up on any readings you've missed.

MANY OF US WILL ADMIT that although we *desire* to do things God's way, we don't always succeed. We think we know what's best. We make decisions based on how we feel, instead of seeking the face of God for clarity and direction. We've all been guilty of it. But in this next season, we've got to do things God's way.

In week 17, when we read the book of 2 Samuel, we saw David learn the hard way to trust in God. Now let's return to that story as it's retold in the book of 1 Chronicles. Israel recaptured the Ark of the Lord from the Philistines and kept it at the house of Abinadab. David wanted to bring it back to Jerusalem, but he did it the wrong way, and Uzzah died as a result. Now the Ark is being kept at the house of Obed-Edom, but it still needs to go back to Jerusalem. This time, however, David wants to do it the right way. He confesses that he and his men failed to ask God how to maneuver His presence, which caused them to lose that presence.

How many times have we failed to recall what God has said about how we should handle a certain situation? How many times have we failed to recall how God said to handle our enemies? How many times have we failed to ask Him how we should make decisions? Countless times, we've failed to gain permission to move the way we moved, and because we went the way that felt right to us, we made errors that we didn't have to make.

Now, in 1 Chronicles 15:26, when David and the elders of Israel went to bring up the Ark from the house of Obed-Edom, the Bible says God *helped* the Levites who were carrying it. You see, the first time, they messed up because they didn't trust God. But this time, they did it God's way, and He gave them the strength to do what they were assigned to do.

We must always be reminded that we simply have to trust God to be our help. Some things seem impossible. Some obstacles seem too hard to overcome. But when we do it God's way, He gives us the strength that we need to overcome and conquer what seems too great for us to accomplish. Sometimes we can forget that there is nothing too hard for God. Sometimes we forget where our help comes from. Doing it God's way means trusting His plan and relying upon His power to be a very present help.

~~~~~~

POINTS TO PONDER

1. What decisions or actions have you had to adjust to doing God's way?

_____

_____

2. Even when you knew God's way was the right way, how difficult was it to make the adjustment?

_____

_____

3. In the very near future, what changes will you make to line up with the ways of God?

_____

_____

THIS IS MY PRAYER

Dear Lord,

Please lead, guide, and direct my paths. I confess that I have not always done things according to Your way, but today I confess my sins, and I thank You for Your forgiveness. Thank You for the opportunity to do it the right way. Thank You for the help and the strength to live life Your way. In Jesus's name, amen.

IT'S PRAYING TIME

DAILY READINGS

- Day 1: 1 Chronicles 23–26
- Day 2: 1 Chronicles 27–29
- Day 3: 2 Chronicles 1–3
- **Day 4: 2 Chronicles 4–7**
- Day 5: 2 Chronicles 8–10
- Day 6: 2 Chronicles 11–13
- Day 7: Catch up on any readings you've missed.

WE LIVE IN A TIME of turbulence. The fact is, we can look at the world and complain about how badly things are going. We may blame the decay of our society on government leaders or sit around and cry, "Woe is me" for all that's going wrong in our communities. However, scripture makes it very clear that no matter what it looks like across this nation, God's people have the power, authority, and responsibility to turn things around through the power of prayer.

In 2 Chronicles 7, we find God answering the prayers of Solomon and the children of Israel. They had just built the temple in Jerusalem, and everything seemed to be going as it should. However, Solomon knew the temperament of the people, so he prayed and asked God to have mercy on the people when they got off track and began to operate in error. He asked God what they should do when times got hard and pestilence and famine hit the land.

It took God a little while to answer, but Solomon kept praying. When God doesn't answer when we think He ought to, we have a tendency to quit praying. But that's not the time to get slack—it's the time to press on in prayer even more. That's what Solomon did. He prayed and made sacrifices to God on the altar for seven days. On the eighth day, he sent the people home.

That very night, God finally spoke to Solomon and said, "I have heard your prayer and have chosen this place for myself as a house of sacrifice" (2 Chronicles 7:12, ESV). He went on to say that if He didn't let the rain fall or sent locusts to devour the land, all the people would have to do is pray. In verse 14, God says, "If my people who are called by my name humble themselves, and pray and seek my face and turn from their wicked ways, then I will hear from heaven and will forgive their sin and heal their land" (ESV). He said He'd do it for them because they're *His* people. He'd chosen them as His own. He knew what was in their hearts, and He'd watch over them and listen for their cry. No matter what they came up against, God would be there, ready to help.

That same promise has been applied to our lives today, but we must do our part. We must pray, humble ourselves, seek His face, and turn from our wicked ways. This passage in 2 Chronicles shows us that after we do our part, He'll heal what has been torn apart. When we do our part, we then have to trust Him to keep His Word concerning our lives. Without a doubt, it's praying time.

POINTS TO PONDER

1. Knowing that we play a part in our answered prayers, what part do you find most difficult?

_____

_____

2. We're told to pray, humble ourselves, and turn from our wicked ways. Is there any one of these that you have knowingly failed to do?

_____

_____

3. Going forward, which area within these mandates will you intentionally make the effort to grow in?

_____

_____

ACTIONS FOR THE WEEK

1. This week, be very intentional in your time of prayer.
2. Make a list of those things you're seeking God for. Include issues regarding family, work, finances, and, most importantly, things to help you grow spiritually.

WEEK 25
YOU HAVE THE POWER

DAILY READINGS

- **Day 1: Proverbs 18–21**
- Day 2: Proverbs 22–24
- Day 3: Proverbs 25–27
- Day 4: Proverbs 28–31
- Day 5: 2 Chronicles 14–16
- Day 6: 2 Chronicles 17–19
- Day 7: Catch up on any readings you've missed.

PROVERBS 18:21 SAYS, "Death and life are in the power of the tongue" (ESV). In the Message version of the Bible, that's translated as "Words kill, words give life; they're either poison or fruit—you choose." In other words, you're going to speak either blessings or curses. Faith or doubt. Victory or defeat. Abundance or lack. Words have a way of giving direction to where and how far you go. They can determine how easy or difficult the journey will be. What kind of words will you speak? Will they be complaints or encouragements? Will they be negative or positive?

Because we live in a world full of negativity, it actually takes work to stay positive. You'd be surprised at the negative things we say without even trying: "These kids are going to drive me crazy," "I'm never going to get that promotion," or "At this age, I'll probably never marry." We get used to what we see and hear, and, without thinking, we begin to regurgitate what we've consumed. We just have to be intentional with the words that come from our mouths. We've got to shift from harmful words to helpful ones, like "I can," "I will," "I am."

However, in order for our vocabulary to change, our mentality has to change. Philippians 2:5 says, "Let this mind be in you which was also in Christ Jesus" (NKJV)—and there was nothing defeated about Jesus. If we are followers of Jesus Christ, we are supposed to follow his example.

This is a learning process for all of us, and we've got to learn how to turn the tables on the enemy and change our vocabulary. Don't get caught in Satan's trap of constantly speaking words of fear and doubt. Regardless of how impossible your circumstances may seem, keep speaking God's Word in faith. Base what you say less on how you feel and more on what God has said. As of today, start speaking life, not death.

We all have experiences that prompt us to feel fear and doubt. But you've got to change what you say, because what we say determines what we think, and what we think determines what we do. As Proverbs reminds us, words really do have that much power, so we must be intentional about how we use them.

POINTS TO PONDER

1. What are some negative words or phrases that we use daily?

_____

_____

2. What are some helpful words or phrases that we need to incorporate into our daily conversations?

_____

_____

3. In what area of life will you intentionally shift your words in an attempt to shift the course of the situation?

_____

_____

VERSE OF THE WEEK

Words satisfy the mind as much as fruit does the stomach; good talk is as gratifying as a good harvest.

Words kill, words give life; they're either poison or fruit—you choose. ▶ **Proverbs 18:20–21 (MSG)**

WE'RE BETTER TOGETHER

DAILY READINGS

Day 1: 2 Chronicles 20–24

Day 2: 2 Chronicles 25–28

Day 3: 2 Chronicles 29–32

Day 4: 2 Chronicles 33–36

Day 5: Psalms 68–72

Day 6: Psalms 73–78

Day 7: Catch up on any readings you've missed.

GOD DOES NOT WANT US to be divided. We see too much division in our families and churches. It is not the will of God that we war against each other. He said in Leviticus 26:8, "Five of you shall chase a hundred, and a hundred of you shall put ten thousand to flight; your enemies shall fall by the sword before you" (NKJV). But to do that, we have to get on the same page and work together. Instead of fighting against each other, it's time to join forces against the enemy of our souls. We get the best results when we do it together.

In 2 Chronicles 20, King Jehoshaphat received word that the kingdom of Judah was about to be invaded by "a great multitude" (verse 2, NKJV) of armies from three different nations. We all have times when we've got things coming at us from all sides, and we don't always know how to handle it. This is where the kingdom of Judah was, and they weren't sure what to do. They could have fallen apart under the pressure and begun to turn on each other, but they had enough sense to know whom to call on. King Jehoshaphat went on a fast and began to pray, seeking the Lord on his nation's behalf. And as soon as he finished praying, he received a word through the prophet Jahaziel: The Lord said they weren't going to have to fight in this battle, because this battle didn't belong to them; it belonged to the Lord.

Nothing gives God more glory than when He can see us working out His plan together. We're not called to be lone rangers. Don't forget, we are many members, but we are one body. It takes us all working together to make some things happen. You may be able to get it done by yourself, but we're so much better when we do it together. The possibilities are limitless as to what God can do through our team efforts.

POINTS TO PONDER

1. What battles are you fighting right now that probably belong to the Lord?

    _____

    _____

2. Looking back, can you say that you possibly lost some battles because you refused to join forces with someone else?

    _____

    _____

3. Going forward, can you think of other team players you can connect with in order to achieve a common goal?

    _____

    _____

FURTHER THOUGHTS FOR THE WEEK

After receiving the Word of the Lord, King Jehoshaphat appointed singers to go ahead of the army and sing praises to God. The moment they began to sing was the very moment that God caused the armies that were against Jehoshaphat to begin to fight each other. When Judah's army arrived at the battleground, they did not have to fight, because all their enemies were already dead. It took them three days to gather all the spoils (goods, clothing, etc.), because it was more than they could carry.

WEEK 27
CALLED FOR SUCH A TIME AS THIS

DAILY READINGS

Day 1: Esther 1–3

Day 2: Esther 4–6

Day 3: Esther 7–10

Day 4: Psalms 79–84

Day 5: Psalms 85–89

Day 6: Psalms 90–96

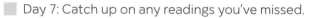

Day 7: Catch up on any readings you've missed.

THE BOOK OF ESTHER is the story of a Jewish girl who was divinely called to go to King Xerxes of Persia and intercede on behalf of an entire people. The Jews were in exile, and after the king of Persia had cast his previous wife out for disobedience, Esther had become queen via a kingdom-wide beauty contest and the help of the Lord. But her cousin and father figure, Mordecai, had made an enemy of the king's adviser Haman, because Mordecai refused to bow down to him (or to anyone but God). So Haman tricked the king into decreeing that all Jews be killed. Mordecai sent word to Esther that all her people were depending on her, but she was reluctant to intercede with her husband the king, who didn't know she was Jewish. The law said that if the king didn't request your presence, you couldn't go before him, or you might be put to death. But in Esther 4:14, Mordecai asked her, "Who knows if perhaps you were made queen for just such a time as this?" The rest, as you'll read this week, is history.

My sister, please know that you, too, have been called for such a time as this. Rest assured that all the things you've been through have prepared you for your now. Every battle you've had to fight and every tear you've shed have been a part of your process. Just as a soldier has to go through training before going to war, you have gone through various trials that have prepared you for this time of your life.

Maybe you're being called as an intercessor for your family because you have experience seeking the Lord. Or you're being called to intercede for your neighborhood, city, or state because you have a sincere desire for peace and unity to be the driving force on earth. Perhaps you're being called to pray for the school system in your region because you have been so fervent in prayer for children over the years. At a time of so much negativity, you're being called to make positivity popular again. At a time when there is so much wickedness and hatred, you're being called to show love. You're being called to help restore faith in humanity. You're being called to be an influence and an example of kindness in the world. Every juncture in your life has prepared you for such a time as this.

~~~~~~

POINTS TO PONDER

1. What do you feel you've been called to do on the earth?

    _____

    _____

2. Have you ever felt reluctant to do something you knew you were called to do? Why?

    _____

    _____

3. If you were assigned to pray for your neighborhood, what would be at the top of your prayer list?

    _____

    _____

FURTHER THOUGHTS FOR THE WEEK

How exactly did Queen Esther triumph? In Esther 7, she invited King Xerxes and Haman to a dinner, where the king said he'd give Esther anything she wanted, even half the kingdom. So Esther pleaded with him to spare her life and the lives of her people. Of course, the king was furious and demanded to know who would dare to want to harm Esther. She exposed Haman as the culprit, and the king had him impaled on the very pole Haman had set up for Mordecai. Haman experienced the repercussions of his own destructive intentions. This just proves that "whatever a man sows, that he will also reap" (Galatians 6:7, NKJV).

WEEK 28
MAINTAIN

DAILY READINGS

Day 1: Job 1–3

Day 2: Job 4–7

Day 3: Job 8–11

Day 4: Job 12–14

Day 5: Job 15–17

Day 6: Job 18–21

Day 7: Catch up on any readings you've missed.

THE BOOK OF JOB is about a man who loved God and hated evil. He lived a successful life. He had seven sons and three daughters. He and his sons were homeowners, owned an abundance of livestock, and were well respected throughout the community. However, there was a conversation taking place in the heavens between God and Satan. Satan thought he could get people to turn their backs on God, even if they were righteous. God asked, "Have you considered My servant Job?" (Job 1:8, NKJV), and Satan did just that. He attacked everything that belonged to Job. Job lost his home, possessions, children, and health—but he didn't lose his faith in God. Job was faced with the ultimate challenge to hold on to his integrity as an upright man even though he was at the lowest point of his life.

When Job went and sat among the ashes to scrape at the boils all over his body with a broken piece of pottery, his wife finally spoke up: "Are you still trying to maintain your integrity? Curse God and die" (Job 2:9). Now, before we look down on her for making this statement, we have to remember that Job wasn't the only one suffering. His wife was suffering in her own way. She was married to him. Everything he lost, she lost. Those were her 10 children who died. That was her house that was destroyed. Now she is watching her husband in pain as his body deteriorates before her eyes. You also have to remember that women had no wealth of their own. Everything this woman had was tied up with this man. She just wanted it all to end, so she told her husband to curse God and get out of this misery.

As a woman, I can empathize with Job's wife. I can't say

that I wouldn't have felt the same in her position. When there is personal loss, anyone's emotions can get the best of them (regardless of gender). However, let me encourage you to do your level best to maintain your focus in the midst of difficult times. Let us take a lesson from Job. No matter what his wife said, no matter what his friends said, no matter what he lost or how he felt, he was determined to maintain his integrity and commitment to God.

Listen, ladies, we must remain determined that no matter what goes on at home or what happens on the job, we've got to hold our positions. Our families, children, and spouses are counting on us to maintain our focus. The devil is cunning. He'll attack your marriage, your children, your wealth, and your body in an effort to make you either give up on life or give up on God. But you must be persuaded to persist in your commitment to God, trusting that He still has a plan for your life. No matter the test, maintain your integrity.

POINTS TO PONDER

1. Attacks come in many ways. Can you think of anything that would cause you to even *think* about turning your back on God?

_____

_____

_____

2. Has there ever been a time in your life when you sincerely wanted to give up? How did you handle it?

_____

_____

_____

3. If you were Job's wife, how would you have encouraged your husband?

_____

_____

_____

_____

VERSE OF THE WEEK

Job scraped his skin with a piece of broken pottery as he sat among the ashes. His wife said to him, "Are you still trying to maintain your integrity? Curse God and die."

But Job replied, "You talk like a foolish woman. Should we accept only good things from the hand of God and never anything bad?" So in all this, Job said nothing wrong. ▶ Job 2:8–10

WEEK 29
YOU HAVE
TO KNOW

DAILY READINGS

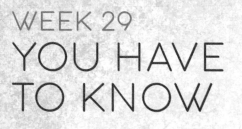

☐ Day 1: Job 22–24

☐ Day 2: Job 25–28

☐ Day 3: Job 29–31

☐ Day 4: Job 32–35

☐ Day 5: Job 36–39

☐ **Day 6: Job 40–42**

☐ Day 7: Catch up on any readings you've missed.

LAST WEEK, we started a discussion about the life of Job. Chapters 1 and 2 tell us of his trials. During his time of suffering, he experienced silence from God. From chapter 2 to chapter 37, Job hears nothing from God. Throughout those chapters, he's criticized by friends he thought he could count on, who believe he must have done something evil to deserve all this. Sometimes, throughout those chapters, he wishes he were dead. But he endures the process until finally God speaks to him, illustrating His power by recounting creation to Job, reminding Job of who He is and what Job doesn't know about Him.

In the last chapter of the book, Job changes his mind about some things. Because of the experiences he's had and because of God's words, Job knows it's time to come clean with God. At this point, he's been suffering for a while, and he wants to make sure his life truly is lining up with God. He desperately needs his life to change, so he decides to change his posture to one of repentance. No longer will he just feel sorry for himself or be angry about his situation. Now he will occupy a position of humility and repentance.

In Job 42:5–6, Job says, "I had only heard about you before, but now I have seen you with my own eyes. I take back everything I said, and I sit in dust and ashes to show my repentance." Job made assumptions and said things he shouldn't have. Several times, he wished he were never born, and he even went as far as wanting to take God to court to plead his case. However, he had to repent, because he realized he allowed others to affect his beliefs about and response to God. He was basically saying, *I really didn't know how sovereign You are, but now I know. I didn't really know You to be a keeper in spite of the struggles, but now I know. I didn't really know You could bless me beyond my circumstances, but now I know.*

We can't afford to base our lives on what others have to say. We simply have to know who's in control of our lives. We have to know that God's Word is still true. His Word cannot come back to Him void. It doesn't matter if He said it 10 years ago; God's got to do what He said. And you've got to know that God is behind the scenes right now, preparing those things that have been stored up for you, even if you've lost everything like Job. It may not fully make sense, but there are just some things you have to know.

POINTS TO PONDER

1. After Job's testing, he went through a season of silence. Have you ever experienced the silence of God? How did you handle it?

2. Struggles can cloud our thoughts. Has there ever been a time when you've trusted what *others* had to say rather than what God has already said?

3. What do you know about God that no one could ever change your mind about?

FURTHER THOUGHTS FOR THE WEEK

Even after all Job's suffering, it's clear that God still had a plan for his prosperity. When Job repented, God restored him and gave him twice as much as he had before. In fact, "the Lord blessed Job in the second half of his life even more than in the beginning" (Job 42:12). Job lived 140 years after his restoration. God blessed him to see four generations of children and grandchildren. He died having lived a long and fulfilled life.

HIS DESTINY, HER PURPOSE

DAILY READINGS

Day 1: John 1–4

Day 2: John 5–8

Day 3: John 9–11

Day 4: John 12–15

Day 5: John 16–18

Day 6: John 19–21

Day 7: Catch up on any readings you've missed.

JOHN 12:1–11 tells the story of a woman who became a role model. Jesus was sitting in the house of Simon the Leper. He was there with his disciples, as well as three siblings: Mary, Martha, and Lazarus. The text says that Mary did something that touched the heart of Jesus and ultimately changed the rest of her life. She didn't waste time talking, asking permission, or making apologies for her actions. She purposed in her heart to anoint Jesus. She wasn't at this gathering just to be sociable. She was prepared to wash the Messiah's feet with expensive perfume and dry them with her hair. She clearly understood His destiny. She understood that He would soon be crucified like a common criminal, and she made it her responsibility to anoint Him, because there was nothing common or criminal about Him. On this particular day, His destiny and her purpose collided. It did not matter that she was a woman. This woman was divinely placed in that spot at that moment for that purpose.

Do you know your purpose? If we are to impact the lives of others, we have to know what we have been purposed to do. Just as He created the sun to shine by day and the moon to shine by night, God has created each of us for a specific purpose. No matter our past or the neighborhood we grew up in, we were created to complete an assignment that only we could complete. Life becomes so much more meaningful when we live it according to our purpose. So whatever your purpose, just do it.

If you know your purpose is to teach and help others learn more about Christ, do it. If your purpose is to start a business to help meet the needs of the low-income community, do it. If your purpose is to evangelize and lead others to Christ, do it. If your purpose is to sing praises unto God, do it. You weren't created to do nothing. You were created to impact the Kingdom of God, and if you are a part of the Kingdom, you were created to be the head and not the tail. You were created to be a leader in society, in the community, and in the church. If you're going to change the lives of those around you, you've got to be confident in who you are and walk in your purpose.

POINTS TO PONDER

1. Do you know what you have been purposed to do?

_____

_____

2. Is there anything that has hindered you from fulfilling that purpose? If so, what?

_____

_____

3. Does your purpose work in conjunction with someone else's purpose? Who and what?

_____

_____

ACTIONS FOR THE WEEK

1. Search your heart and determine what you have been created to do.

2. Come up with a plan and begin to implement a portion of that plan.

3. If your purpose works in conjunction with others, schedule a call or meeting this week to discuss the potential process.

4. Plan how you will begin to fulfill your purpose over the course of the next 30 days.

WEEK 31
DUE SEASON

DAILY READINGS

Day 1: Ecclesiastes 1–4

Day 2: Ecclesiastes 5–8

Day 3: Ecclesiastes 9–12

Day 4: Psalms 97–100

Day 5: Psalms 101–103

Day 6: Psalms 104–106

Day 7: Catch up on any readings you've missed.

THE BOOK OF ECCLESIASTES consists of poetic writings by King Solomon. He starts off by saying that every activity under the sun has an appointed time. In Ecclesiastes 3:2–8, each verse notes a characteristic activity of life matched with its opposite. Just as surely as something good happens, something bad can and will happen as well. Just as surely as day comes, night is sure to arrive. Just as surely as summer comes, stick around and you'll see winter soon. That's the way God ordained it. By the same token, nobody wants to suffer or be in need, but it unfortunately will happen. Nonetheless, the good news is that it won't last. As 1 Peter 1:6 says, "In this you greatly rejoice, though now for a little while, if need be, you have been grieved by various trials" (NKJV). But guess what? It's only for a season.

So, while we're waiting on our season of grace and favor, we have to keep in mind that whatever happens is in God's plan. God has allowed it all for a purpose. We have to learn how to accept God's timetable, and we've got to trust that He knows exactly what He's doing. Ecclesiastes 3:9–11 says, "What do people really get for all their hard work? I have seen the burden God has placed on us all. Yet God has made everything beautiful for its own time. He has planted eternity in the human heart, but even so, people cannot see the whole scope of God's work from beginning to end." Truth is, we'll never be able to understand the mind of God. He is infinite in His wisdom, and our minds could never possibly understand His ways. We have no idea what God will do or how He's going to do it. We just have to trust His timing and His plan.

If you can just make it through one season, you'll eventually embrace the next. If you can get through the season of lack, God will shift you into a season of overflow. If you can make it through the season of sickness, God will shift you into a season of good health. If you can get through the season of silence, God will shift you into a season of revelation. But you've got to trust God through this season. Don't be discouraged, and by all means, do not despair. Recall what Paul wrote in Galatians 6:9: "Let us not grow weary while doing good, for in due season we shall reap if we do not lose heart" (NKJV). No matter the season you're in right now, get through it so that you can get to your due season.

~~~~~~

POINTS TO PONDER

1. Understanding that there are various seasons of life, what is the most difficult to accept about the hard seasons?

_____

_____

_____

_____

2. How have you handled your hard seasons in the past?

_____

_____

_____

_____

3. Going forward, what will you do differently when your seasons begin to change?

_____

_____

_____

_____

VERSE OF THE WEEK

For everything there is a season, a time for every activity under heaven. A time to be born and a time to die. A time to plant and a time to harvest. A time to kill and a time to heal. A time to tear down and a time to build up. A time to cry and a time to laugh. A time to grieve and a time to dance. A time to scatter stones and a time to gather stones. A time to embrace and a time to turn away. A time to search and a time to quit searching. A time to keep and a time to throw away.

▶ **Ecclesiastes 3:1–6**

WEEK 32
OH, WHAT LOVE!

DAILY READINGS

Day 1: Song of Songs 1–4

Day 2: Song of Songs 5–8

Day 3: Psalms 107–110

Day 4: Psalms 111–116

Day 5: Psalms 117–119

Day 6: Psalms 120–128

Day 7: Catch up on any readings you've missed.

THE SONG OF SONGS is a collection of love poems told from the perspective of two individuals who are desperately in love with one another. Their desire for each other is obvious in their descriptions, which are so specific you can sense the sexual tension between them. The man says to his beloved, "Your lips are like scarlet ribbon; your mouth is inviting. Your cheeks are like rosy pomegranates behind your veil. . . . Your breasts are like two fawns, twin fawns of a gazelle grazing among the lilies" (Song of Songs 4:3–5). But he confirms that this love goes beyond physical attraction: "For love is as strong as death, its jealousy as enduring as the grave. Love flashes like fire, the brightest kind of flame. Many waters cannot quench love, nor can rivers drown it. If a man tried to buy love with all his wealth, his offer would be utterly scorned" (8:6–7). Love is dangerous and life-giving at the same time. Love hurts, but it also restores. These poems reveal just how complicated and yet satisfying love is. And at the end of the day, love is a gift from God, who is complex, loving, satisfying, and so much more.

Many say that these writings are actually allegorical and that the romance is symbolic of the love God demonstrated for His children. It shows how He loved us so passionately that He gave a portion of Himself when He sent His Son to die on a cross. How interesting that the metaphor used to express that is a beautiful love story! Who doesn't like a good love story? If you're like me, ladies, you cherish the thought of someone loving you completely and unconditionally. (Men do, too!) Most women I know would love their significant others to pay such close attention to them, describing their appearance with such passionate, flowery words. The Song of Songs causes one to long for that kind of love.

Well, believe it or not, that's how God loves us. He loves us so passionately and completely that He sacrificed His only Son for our sins. Many of us denied Him and even ran from Him, but He loved us so much that He chased after us and proved His love. So if there's ever a time when you're feeling devoid of love, think about the Song of Songs and God's amazing love! Oh, what love!

POINTS TO PONDER

1. If you had to describe your love for God, how would you describe it?

   _____

   _____

2. If you had to convince someone else of God's love for them, how would you share His love?

   _____

   _____

3. How has God shown His love toward you in the past week?

   _____

   _____

   _____

ACTION FOR THE WEEK

Take a moment and really think about your love relationship with the Lord. Then take some time and write your love story. How did you meet? What were the circumstances surrounding your first encounter? When did you finally decide to come into a covenant relationship with Him? How do you intend to prove your continued love to Him?

WEEK 33
I'M NOT WORTHY, BUT I'LL GO

DAILY READINGS

- Day 1: Isaiah 1–4
- **Day 2: Isaiah 5–8**
- Day 3: Isaiah 9–12
- Day 4: Isaiah 13–16
- Day 5: Isaiah 17–20
- Day 6: Isaiah 21–24
- Day 7: Catch up on any readings you've missed.

IN ISAIAH 6, we read of how Isaiah was called to be a prophet. It happened in the year King Uzziah died (740 BC). It was not until this time that Isaiah was finally in a position to walk in complete obedience to God and hear from Him directly.

Isaiah testifies that one day, he saw God in a vision, seated on a throne with the train of His robe filling the temple. There were angels around him singing, "Holy, holy, holy is the Lord of hosts; the whole earth is full of his glory!" (Isaiah 6:3, ESV). God's presence was so powerful that the doorposts began to shake and smoke filled the temple. It was so powerful that Isaiah immediately began to see his flaws, and when he took a good look at himself, he didn't feel worthy to be in God's presence. He said, "Woe is me! For I am lost; for I am a man of unclean lips, and I dwell in the midst of a people of unclean lips" (6:5, ESV). In other words: *I do things I shouldn't do. I say things I shouldn't say. Why would God take the time to touch somebody like me?* He knew he could never measure up to God's standard of holiness.

You see, when you have a real encounter with God, He'll allow you to see yourself. He'll allow you to see your sin. When we really get in His presence and look at ourselves in the light of God's perfect holiness, we see the truth about ourselves. And that's hard to do. It's hard to admit we've done wrong and gotten out of the will of God. But if you're ever going to get in a position where you can help somebody else, you've got to be honest with yourself. Admit that you have shortcomings; you have some ways about you that need changing. Nobody is perfect, and we never will be, as long as we're in this flesh. However, we all need an encounter with God to cleanse us and prepare us to minister to those we've been called to.

There is somebody assigned to you. There is somebody who's going to be saved because of what you say, who's going to be delivered because of what comes from you. There is somebody, somewhere, waiting on your testimony. Despite his "unclean lips," Isaiah became one of the greatest prophets ever known. As imperfect as we are, God loves us, and He can and will use us for His glory.

POINTS TO PONDER

1. Has there ever been a time in your life when you didn't feel worthy to render service unto the Lord or His people? Why?

_____

_____

_____

2. Have you ever had an Isaiah encounter? What were the circumstances surrounding that encounter?

_____

_____

_____

3. Everybody is called to somebody. To whom do you think you're called?

_____

_____

_____

VERSE OF THE WEEK

He touched my lips with it and said, "See, this coal has touched your lips. Now your guilt is removed, and your sins are forgiven."

Then I heard the Lord asking, "Whom should I send as a messenger to this people? Who will go for us?"

I said, "Here I am. Send me." ▸ Isaiah 6:7–8

WEEK 34
YOUR NEXT
IS NOW

DAILY READINGS

Day 1: Isaiah 25–27

Day 2: Isaiah 28–31

Day 3: Isaiah 32–35

Day 4: Isaiah 36–39

Day 5: Isaiah 40–42

Day 6: Isaiah 43–46

Day 7: Catch up on any readings you've missed.

WHEN WE LOOK AT THE PROPHETIC WRITINGS of Isaiah, we find God speaking through the prophet, reminding His people that He is the Almighty God and besides Him there is no other. He confirms over and over again that He is the one in full control of our lives. And He tells the nation of Judah, "Do not remember the former things, nor consider the things of old" (Isaiah 43:18, NKJV).

God was encouraging the people of Judah not to dwell on how they had to struggle in the past to become a nation. He's saying that same thing to us today. God doesn't want you dwelling on the past, because when you do, you'll find yourself still feeling some of the hurt, anger, and pain. We can appreciate the past. We can learn from it. But we can't stay stuck there. Isaiah 43:18 in the Message translation of the Bible says, "Forget about what's happened; don't keep going over old history." Jesus even says in Luke 9:62 that "no one, having put his hand to the plow, and looking back, is fit for the kingdom of God" (NKJV).

So you've got to ask God to help you forge ahead. The past has got to be the past so God can shift you to the next phase of your journey. So often, we can get too comfortable and complacent, but there comes a time when you have to move toward that next phase of your journey, whether it be from hourly employee to management, from traveling evangelist to a pastoral position, or from the single life to marriage and motherhood.

You have to be open to the next phase to get there. Your mind has to be prepared for it. You've got to motivate and position yourself for it. And you've got to know that there is something greater for you there. I don't know about anybody else, but I'm ready for the more of God. I don't want to be stuck, and I don't want to be stagnant. If He has a next place, I'm ready for it. We can't grieve forever about what was. It's time to move on. It's time to move forward. And if that's you today, I want you to know that your next begins now!

POINTS TO PONDER

1. What do you believe the next phase of your journey looks like?

   _____

   _____

2. What is something that has kept you stagnant and complacent?

   _____

   _____

3. What strategy will you put in place to help move you to your next phase?

   _____

   _____

THIS IS MY PRAYER

Dear Lord,
Help me forget the former things and keep the past in the past. Help me keep my eyes on You as I move forward in this next phase of life with You. Give me clarity and an understanding of Your will. Help me embrace the new thing as I trust You every step of the way. Give me strategy and give me strength to do everything You assign my hands to do. In Jesus's name, amen.

WEEK 35
THINK BIG

DAILY READINGS

Day 1: Isaiah 47—49

Day 2: Isaiah 50—53

Day 3: Isaiah 54—57

Day 4: Isaiah 58—60

Day 5: Isaiah 61—63

Day 6: Isaiah 64—66

Day 7: Catch up on any readings you've missed.

IN ISAIAH 54, we find God speaking to a people who had been exiled to Babylon and left there for 70 years. He calls them barren because they had spent many years not living up to their promise; they were spiritually stuck in a rut and unable to prosper. They had been promised a future of abundance, but at this point, they were fruitless in the church of God's Kingdom.

What do you do when you know you're supposed to be doing more than what you're doing? What do you do when you know you're not operating at your potential? A spiritual rut can leave you feeling defeated, stuck, and stagnant. You have all the tools, but the tools aren't working for you. You know you have what it takes, but you have nothing to show for it. What do you do?

Isaiah told the children of Israel to start making preparations based on their promise. Even though they were in exile, he told them to prepare with their future in mind instead of settling for what they had right then. In order to do that, they had to refuse to be limited by their present status. They had to see their potential and work toward that.

That's a lesson for us as well. We've got to stop limiting ourselves and start reaching beyond our normal limitations. My sister, you will never know how much you can accomplish until you stretch yourself. You've got to change the way you see yourself. You've got to start thinking bigger. Your present life circumstances should not hinder your dreams and desires for better or greater things.

The truth is, ladies, we hold ourselves back. We think we can't accomplish certain things because our present status doesn't look like we think it should. We might think we can't start a business because we don't have enough money on hand, or that we can't be a homeowner because we don't have the best credit scores. But for those who have the capacity to believe, God is enlarging your capacity to receive.

Even though the children of Israel were in the worst possible situation, exiled in Babylon, God was offering them a glimpse of where they were going. That goes for you, too. Make room for who and what He's sending your way. You're used to living in your small space, but this next season is not only about you. It's about the responsibility He's about to entrust you with for that job. It's about the larger platform He's preparing with you in mind. Start putting those plans together now, but don't plan with only yourself in mind. Plan with expansion in mind. Think big.

POINTS TO PONDER

1. Have you ever experienced a barren season in your life? In what way?

_____

_____

_____

_____

2. In what ways have you been underestimating or limiting yourself?

_____

_____

_____

_____

3. What is that big thing that God is placing into your hands?

_____

_____

_____

_____

VERSE OF THE WEEK

**"Sing, barren woman, who has never had a baby. Fill the air with
song, you who've never experienced childbirth! You're ending up
with far more children than all those childbearing women." God
says so! . . . "Don't be afraid—you're not going to be embarrassed.
Don't hold back—you're not going to come up short."**
▸ Isaiah 54:1–4 (MSG)

PRAYER STILL WORKS

DAILY READINGS

☐ Day 1: Acts 1–3

☐ Day 2: Acts 4–7

☐ Day 3: Acts 8–10

☐ **Day 4: Acts 11–14**

☐ Day 5: Acts 15–17

☐ Day 6: Acts 18–21

☐ Day 7: Catch up on any readings you've missed.

IN ACTS 12, we find Peter in jail, hours away from execution. He was bound by chains between two sleeping soldiers so that if he moved, they'd wake up. The prison doors were locked and bolted, with more soldiers at the door to make sure no one could rescue him. But an angel of the Lord came to Peter and woke him. When the angel touched him, his chains fell off. Then he was told to put on his clothes and follow the angel wherever he led. They passed the first two sets of guards, and then they came upon an iron gate that would surely stop them. But how many know that God can do the impossible? God met Peter at his very point of need and opened up those iron gates.

Once Peter was safely on the streets, the angel left him. Peter then went to Mary's house, where people were praying for him. When he knocked at the door, a young girl came and asked who was there. He told her who he was, and she recognized his voice because she had heard him pray and preach. But instead of letting him in, she went and told the others, who thought that someone was playing a trick on them. Peter was in jail—it couldn't be him on the other side of the door. Despite the fact that they'd been praying, they had a hard time believing. They told the girl she was crazy. It couldn't be Peter. Peter was in jail; it must have been his angel.

This is a lesson for us all. When we pray, we must believe what we're praying. We can't pray with faith and doubt at the same time. A lot of us pray about a certain thing but then allow the spirit of doubt to cloud our prayers. Or we'll ask God to do the hard thing, but then we'll believe that it's much too hard to come to pass. Quite the contrary, when we pray, we must believe that there is absolutely nothing too hard for God. According to Ephesians 3:20, God is "able to do exceedingly abundantly above all that we ask or think" (NKJV). Whatever you can speak or imagine, our God is able to do that and more.

So be encouraged and don't stop praying. I don't care how long you've been praying or how difficult it may seem. I know there are times when we get discouraged because it seems like God doesn't hear our prayers. But I want to encourage your hearts today and tell you that He hears and He will answer. Your prayers are not in vain. Prayer worked for Peter when he was in jail. Prayer still works.

POINTS TO PONDER

1. What is that thing you've been praying about that seems impossible?

_____

_____

_____

_____

2. Why is it so difficult to believe that God is able to do those hard things?

_____

_____

_____

_____

3. What does your prayer regimen look like? Do you have a routine, or is your prayer time sporadic?

_____

_____

_____

_____

ACTION FOR THE WEEK

Be intentional this week during your time of prayer. Take a day to commit to pray for these people:

1. Family (spouse, children, siblings, parents)

2. Friends

3. Church family

4. Coworkers

5. Community

6. Government leaders

7. Yourself!

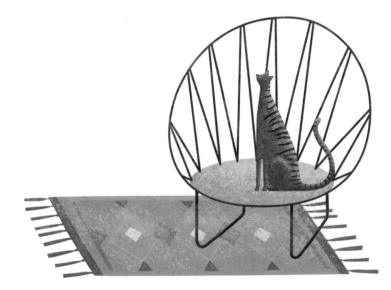

WEEK 37
YOU WILL
MAKE IT

DAILY READINGS

Day 1: Acts 22–25

Day 2: Acts 26–28

Day 3: Jeremiah 1–3

Day 4: Jeremiah 4–6

Day 5: Jeremiah 7–11

Day 6: Jeremiah 12–15

Day 7: Catch up on any readings you've missed.

IN ACTS 27, we find the story of Paul's journey in a ship and how the Lord strategically maneuvered a terrible storm to work for Paul's good. Paul had been arrested for preaching the gospel and was being taken across the Mediterranean to stand trial in Rome. The journey by sea was difficult, and Paul tried to convince his captors not to keep sailing, but they didn't listen. A storm hit and got worse and worse for three days, to the point that the people on the ship began throwing cargo overboard to lighten the load.

The other prisoners and soldiers began to fear for their lives, but Paul shared with them a word from the Lord. He told them an angel had appeared to him and told him not to be afraid, because he and everyone sailing with him would make it to their destination. He told them to take courage, because he trusted God to do what He said. I'm sure it was difficult for them to trust the word of a prisoner, but at that point, what choice did they have?

After being tossed to and fro for 14 days, they were finally shipwrecked, and parts of the ship began to break up in the water. The soldiers considered killing the prisoners so they couldn't escape, but Paul let them know that if they did that, they themselves wouldn't survive. You see, Paul knew the grace that was over his life. He knew that as long as he was on board, they would all make it to safety, because the Lord had told him they would. So the officer told everybody who could swim to go ahead and swim for it, while everybody else was to find a plank or other piece of wood to help them float to safety.

Maybe there have been times when you've experienced a shipwreck in your life. I'm sure there have been times when you felt like you would drown under all the pressure—but you're still here. Maybe you didn't have the strength to swim, but you still made it to shore on those broken pieces of the ship. The fact is, what you thought would take you under has been the very thing to get you where you are right now. That shipwreck was terrifying, but it brought you to your destined place. You survived it all, and you made it to the other side because of the promise that's over your life.

Maybe you've been through a storm, are in the midst of a storm, or are getting ready to go through a storm. Whatever the case, you will make it! Because of the One who watches over your life, you will survive!

POINTS TO PONDER

1. Have you experienced a time in your life when it felt like you were in the midst of a storm? How did you handle it?

_____

_____

_____

2. Today, when we're notified of an impending storm, we know how to prepare for it. If you knew you were on the verge of a spiritual storm, how would you prepare for it?

_____

_____

_____

3. When you experience storms in your life, are you encouraged or discouraged by them? Why?

_____

_____

_____

_____

THIS IS MY PRAYER

Dear Lord,

Help me trust You at all times, during the sunshine and in the midst of the storm. I admit that I don't always understand Your way, but help me always trust Your plan. Keep me ever mindful that it won't always be this way, because of the promises You've made concerning me. Help me remain steadfast in my commitment to You as I remain unwavering in my faith. In Jesus's name, amen.

GOD
KEPT ME

DAILY READINGS

☐ **Day 1: Jeremiah 16–19**

☐ Day 2: Jeremiah 20–22

☐ Day 3: Jeremiah 23–26

☐ Day 4: Jeremiah 27–30

☐ Day 5: Jeremiah 31–34

☐ Day 6: Jeremiah 35–37

☐ Day 7: Catch up on any readings you've missed.

IN JEREMIAH 18, God told the prophet Jeremiah to go down to the potter's house because He had something to show him. Jeremiah was discouraged about what he saw in the people of Judah, because no matter how much he preached and prophesied, they just weren't getting it. They were determined to do what they wanted to do: sin and worship idols. The Lord wanted to help Jeremiah and bring some understanding to the matter, so He told Jeremiah to go to the potter's house and watch how he worked.

Jeremiah obeyed the Lord's instructions and saw the potter working with a piece of clay. However, the clay got "marred" (verse 4, NKJV), and the project he was working on didn't turn out the way he hoped it would. The Hebrew word for "marred" is *nishkhat*, which means "spoiled," "ruined," or "corrupt." So the clay the potter was working on became spoiled. It was ruined. But what did the potter do? He didn't throw it away. He kept it and made it into another vessel.

When we look back over our lives, that's what God has done for us. He has kept us. Yes, we can be like that piece of clay sometimes. We spin out of control. We become corrupt. We're spoiled, tainted, and in many ways ruined. Because of our sinful nature, we are flawed beings. But in spite of our errors and flaws, God keeps us, because He loves us. We are sometimes rebellious and always subject to error. However, God in His sovereignty does not throw us away. Instead, because of the saving grace of His Son, Jesus, we are remade for the Master's use. He keeps us, scoops us up, and makes us into another vessel.

POINTS TO PONDER

1. Have you ever experienced a time in your life when you knew you were spinning out of control? Explain.

_____

_____

2. In hindsight, can you see how God's grace was covering you during that time? Explain.

_____

_____

_____

3. If you had to testify about who you are versus who you were at that time, what would that testimony sound like?

_____

_____

_____

VERSE OF THE WEEK

The word which came to Jeremiah from the Lord, saying: "Arise and go down to the potter's house, and there I will cause you to hear My words." Then I went down to the potter's house, and there he was, making something at the wheel. And the vessel that he made of clay was marred in the hand of the potter; so he made it again into another vessel, as it seemed good to the potter to make.
▶ **Jeremiah 18:1–4 (NKJV)**

WEEK 39
PURPOSE AND PROCESS

DAILY READINGS

Day 1: Jeremiah 38–41

Day 2: Jeremiah 42–45

Day 3: Jeremiah 46–49

Day 4: Jeremiah 50–52

Day 5: Lamentations 1–2

Day 6: Lamentations 3–5

Day 7: Catch up on any readings you've missed.

IN JEREMIAH 38, we see Jeremiah going through a very difficult time. He was in jail for delivering the Word of the Lord, but he didn't let that stop him. He continued to prophesy and tell the people of the destruction that was soon to come if they didn't repent. The king's men asked permission to put Jeremiah in a dungeon; he was already in prison, but they still felt he was too much of a threat. So they put him in a cistern—a large, rock-lined hole in the ground designed to collect rainwater. It would have been dark, cold, damp, and full of mud. Jeremiah could have died of exposure or starvation.

When they lowered Jeremiah into the hole, scripture does not indicate that Jeremiah said anything to the men. It doesn't say that he tried to put up a fight, plead his case, or beg for his life. What he did, according to the book of Lamentations, was cry out to God: "I called on your name, Lord, from the depths of the pit. You heard my plea: 'Do not close your ears to my cry for relief.' You came near when I called you, and you said, 'Do not fear'" (Lamentations 3:55–57, NIV). This indicates that Jeremiah submitted to the process and held on to his faith. He knew he was doing the right thing, and yet he found himself in this dark place in his life. And what did he do? He cried out to God.

Like Jeremiah, many of us have, at times, found ourselves in a dark place. I admit that I haven't always handled that place very well. But I've learned that I have to submit to God's process. And when those days seem unbearable, I've learned that my peace comes when I cry out to God and release all my cares to Him. I've had to learn that if God has allowed me to be in that space, He has a purpose for it.

Your process may or may not be as difficult as Jeremiah's, but you must learn to submit to it. Why? That process is the tool that God will use to build your discipline and maturity. It's the means by which God will equip you for the career that's being prepared for you, or for your next level of ministry. It doesn't always feel good, but it works for your good. And if you can endure the process, you'll soon see the purpose of it all.

POINTS TO PONDER

1. If you've ever found yourself in a dark place, how did you handle it?

_____

_____

_____

2. While you were going through your process, did you always see it as process? How did that time of your life equip or prepare you?

_____

_____

_____

3. Can you identify the purpose that was attached to your process?

_____

_____

_____

VERSE OF THE WEEK

My enemies, whom I have never harmed, hunted me down like a bird. They threw me into a pit and dropped stones on me. The water rose over my head, and I cried out, "This is the end!" But I called on your name, Lord, from deep within the pit. You heard me when I cried, "Listen to my pleading! Hear my cry for help!" Yes, you came when I called; you told me, "Do not fear." ▸ Lamentations 3:52–57

WEEK 40
JUST SPEAK IT

DAILY READINGS

Day 1: Ezekiel 1–3

Day 2: Ezekiel 4–7

Day 3: Ezekiel 8–11

Day 4: Ezekiel 12–15

Day 5: Ezekiel 16–18

Day 6: Ezekiel 19–21

Day 7: Catch up on any readings you've missed.

EVERYBODY HAS SOMEONE assigned to their life. If you're a mother, your children are assigned to you. If you're a teacher, your students are assigned to you. If you're a minister, you have countless persons of all ages assigned to you. If you're a beautician, you have regular customers who look forward to their time with you each week or each month. Your assignment concerning them is to be a positive example and share with them the knowledge that's been given to you so that they have what they need to become their best selves. That is a major part of our purpose: to give to others what has been given to us.

Unfortunately, what we offer is not always readily received. Sometimes people will listen, sometimes they won't. Sometimes your children will listen, sometimes they won't. But that doesn't stop you from telling them right from wrong. You're still obligated to teach them and show them a better way. Any pastor will tell you that they're almost never sure whether their congregants listen to what is said from the pulpit. But whether or not the congregation receives what's being said, the pastor is still obligated to teach and preach the Word of the Lord.

In Ezekiel 2, Ezekiel received instructions regarding this very principle. Ezekiel's assignment was to go and speak the Word of God to Israel. The problem was that God knew Israel wouldn't be receptive. God told Ezekiel that Israel was stubborn and rebellious and that they wouldn't listen. He said, in fact, that they'd reject Ezekiel's message so harshly that it would sting. But, although Israel would be rebellious, Ezekiel couldn't be. No matter the obstacles, he was still obligated to do and say what he'd been assigned. If he failed to do so, Israel's blood would be on his hands.

When I think of Ezekiel's assignment, I think of the assignments many of us have. It is imperative that we deliver, but we are not always received. We are sometimes met with rebellion, negativity, and closed minds. No matter what you do, you just can't seem to get through to them, whether it's that teenager who refuses to listen, that mentee who wants to go her own way, or that sibling who is determined to do the opposite of everything you say. The rejection may hurt you at your core, because you only want what's best for them and you see them going down a road of destruction. What do you do?

Continue to speak truth. Continue to speak God's Word. Continue to encourage, empower, train, and equip through the Word of God. Hold fast to your assignment, because it's not about what *you* want to do; it's about what *He* wants to do through you. It's about His message and the person to whom He wants it delivered. So speak it when they want to hear it and when they don't. Speak it whether it's embraced or rejected. Just speak His truth.

POINTS TO PONDER

1. Do you know to whom and what you have been assigned?

_____

_____

_____

_____

2. Has there ever been a time when you've felt that what you were offering was being met with rejection? How did you handle the rejection?

_____

_____

_____

_____

3. Has there ever been a time when you allowed your fear to be greater than the assignment? How did you overcome the fear?

_____

_____

_____

_____

THIS IS MY PRAYER

Dear Lord,

Help me always do what You have entrusted to me to do. Help me always remain consistent in my commitment to You. Help me not be fearful, but help me walk, talk, and move in faith. Father, it is my desire to please You and someday hear You say, "Well done." In Jesus's name, amen.

WEEK 41
LESSON
LEARNED

DAILY READINGS

Day 1: Ezekiel 22–24

Day 2: Ezekiel 25–28

Day 3: Ezekiel 29–32

Day 4: Ezekiel 33–36

Day 5: Ezekiel 37–39

Day 6: Ezekiel 40–42

Day 7: Catch up on any readings you've missed.

MOTHERS ARE SAID to be a child's first teacher. Much of what a child knows and how a child acts is a direct result of what the child learns by watching their parents. As children grow, they begin to learn things at school, but there are some lessons that cannot be taught in a classroom. There are some lessons that only life can teach you. If you're like me, you've probably learned some valuable lessons that have only made you better. It might have been tough, but everything was designed to teach you something to help you in your next season of life. Some things were necessary to push you to activate your faith.

In Ezekiel 37:1, the prophet Ezekiel says, "The hand of the Lord was upon me, and he brought me out in the Spirit of the Lord and set me down in the middle of the valley; it was full of bones" (ESV). In this text, the prophet of God was called to another place in the Spirit where God allowed him to see and experience a valley full of dry bones. Now, God could have found any other way to speak to Ezekiel and show him what he needed to know, but he chose to set him down in the middle of a strange and frightening place. He chose this valley of dry bones as the classroom.

The good news is that even when God sets you in a valley, His hand is still upon you. And that's a very valuable lesson to learn. I had to learn that even when I felt like I was going through the valley by myself, I was never alone, because God was always there. There is a blessed assurance in knowing that God is there leading, guiding, and ordering our footsteps.

Verse 4 says, "Prophesy over these bones, and say to them, O dry bones, hear the word of the Lord" (ESV). God purposely set Ezekiel in this dry place and then told him to speak a word. God allows the valleys in our lives to push us to trust His Word at another level. He has to teach us that the Word of God is life to us. It strengthens us when we're weak. It pushes us when we're tired and worn. And He will sometimes test us in that dry place to see whether we'll hold fast to His Word.

There are days when you have to tell yourself that all things are still working together for your good. You have to tell yourself that by the stripes of Jesus you are healed. And what you may not realize is that while you're speaking the Word over your life like Ezekiel spoke the Word over the dry bones, you're being equipped to speak life to others you'll encounter along the way.

POINTS TO PONDER

1. What was one of the most valuable life lessons you had to learn, and why was it so important?

_____

_____

2. Whenever you find yourself in a dry place, how do you respond to it?

_____

_____

3. If your peace of mind were contingent upon one scripture, what would that scripture be, and why?

_____

_____

THIS IS MY PRAYER

Dear Lord,
I'm thankful for every valley and every lesson learned. Thank You for helping me see the value in each valley. Thank You for Your guidance and for consistently ordering my footsteps in Your Word. Help me always remember that when no one else is there, You will always be there to comfort and keep me each and every day. In Jesus's name, amen.

WEEK 42
I KNOW
WHO I AM

DAILY READINGS

☐ Day 1: Ezekiel 43–45

☐ Day 2: Ezekiel 46–48

☐ **Day 3: Daniel 1–4**

☐ Day 4: Daniel 5–8

☐ Day 5: Daniel 9–12

☐ Day 6: Psalms 129–135

☐ Day 7: Catch up on any readings you've missed.

DANIEL 3 TELLS THE STORY of three Jewish boys who took a stand and dared to be different. They refused to bow down and worship an idol. Although they were threatened and persecuted, they made up their minds to follow God.

When the Jews were exiled in Babylon, Daniel found favor with King Nebuchadnezzar. He asked the king to put his three friends, Shadrach, Meshach, and Abednego, in positions of power in the government. But the young men didn't know that with that promotion came some responsibilities they weren't willing to take on: They were told to bow down to a golden statue, and if they refused, they'd be thrown into a fiery furnace. It was a life-or-death decision. Either they were going to give in to the pressure, or they were going to stand their ground. Either they would disobey God's commands, or they would stand on what they believed. What would you do?

When we look at this text, we see that when the king's musicians began to play, everybody began to bow down and worship the golden image just as they were told—everybody but Shadrach, Meshach, and Abednego. These young men knew exactly who they were and whose they were. They were determined to serve God and God alone, and nobody would be able to change their minds. Although the Babylonians could change the young men's names (their Hebrew names were Hananiah, Mishael, and Azariah), they could not change their character. They could not change who they were in God. They were rooted and grounded in their relationship with God.

That's how we have to be, too. We have to know who we are and whose we are. We have to teach our children the same. No matter what others may call us, we know that we are children of the Most High God. We have to always remember that we are "a chosen generation, a royal priesthood, a holy nation, His own special people, that you may proclaim the praises of Him who called you out of darkness into His marvelous light" (1 Peter 2:9, NKJV).

What happened when Shadrach, Meshach, and Abednego refused to bow down before the idol? They were thrown into a fiery furnace "heated seven times hotter than usual"—so hot, in fact, that "the flames killed the soldiers as they threw the three men in" (Daniel 3:19, 22). But God was on their side, and not only were the young men not harmed, the Bible says that "not a hair on their heads was singed" and "they didn't even smell of smoke" (Daniel 3:27). Sometimes, when we're faced with great difficulties, we find it hard to believe that we can make it, because of what we see with our natural eyes. But in spite of it all, we have to believe that we can survive and come out victorious.

POINTS TO PONDER

1. Can you remember as a child being pressured to do something that was not in your heart to do? What was it, and how did you handle it?

_____

_____

_____

_____

2. What advice would you give to young people today who are being faced with peer pressure to go along with the crowd?

_____

_____

_____

_____

FURTHER THOUGHTS FOR THE WEEK

It is every mother's hope to raise children who are confident and sure of themselves. It is every parent's joy to know that you have raised a child who doesn't succumb to pressure to do something that's not within their heart to do. That child has those convictions because they have a mom who has faced similar tests and pressures. The same God who was with you will be with your child. If you are a mother or someone who teaches or mentors others, as you read, don't just think about how you can prepare *yourself* for victory over the fiery furnaces in your life—think about how you can prepare your children or students for theirs as well.

WEEK 43
HIS MERCY
ENDURES

DAILY READINGS

Day 1: Psalms 136–142

Day 2: Psalms 143–150

Day 3: Romans 1–4

Day 4: Romans 5–8

Day 5: Romans 9–12

Day 6: Romans 13–16

Day 7: Catch up on any readings you've missed.

IN PSALM 136, David writes a song of thanksgiving and urges the believer to honor God always by being thankful for His goodness and mercy toward us. David remembers a God who protected, provided for, and pardoned him on many occasions, and he writes a song honoring his God who showed him mercy over and over again. David also speaks of how God remembered and delivered the children of Israel from the hands of Pharaoh. That's why he could say that God's mercy continues to endure.

Many of us could sing this same song each and every day when we think about how good and gracious God has been to us throughout the years—when we think of how He allowed the single mother to successfully raise those children alone, how He allowed you to go back to school and get your degree, or how He favored you with a comfortable home. You can honestly praise God because His mercy has endured in your life.

The fact is, there are a lot of things that we could complain about! But in spite of it all, God has been good to us. We have life. We can still inhale and exhale. That's reason enough to be thankful. David lets us know that when we think of all the things God has done, we should give Him thanks. It doesn't have to be for big things like a raise or a brand-new car. Be thankful for all things—for the sun, moon, and stars.

David said that we should be thankful because God's mercy endures forever—and he knew all about God's mercy. David was an adulterer who slept with another man's wife and had her husband killed on the front line of battle. But God still favored David and anointed him. God had mercy on him and forgave him. Like David, many of us have been witnesses of God's mercy. He's continuously looked past our faults. He had mercy on us and didn't cut us off. David says we ought to be thankful for that.

No matter where you are in life, no matter what's going on around you, you still have a reason to be thankful. Be thankful that in spite of everything, God loves us. Be thankful that He has protected, provided for, and pardoned us time and time again. Be thankful that His mercy endures forever.

POINTS TO PONDER

1. What is your personal definition of mercy?

_____

_____

2. If you had to name three things you're thankful for that *didn't* have to do with money, what would those things be?

_____

_____

3. Have you ever found yourself in a space where you can admit that you were ungrateful or failed to be thankful? Explain.

_____

_____

ACTION FOR THE WEEK

Begin a list of at least three things you're thankful for, and make thanksgiving a part of your prayer time each day. Add three more things to your list each day. By the end of the week, your time of prayer should be filled with more thanksgivings than petitions.

GOD IS MAKING IT UP TO YOU

DAILY READINGS

Day 1: Hosea 1–5

Day 2: Hosea 6–10

Day 3: Hosea 11–14

Day 4: Joel 1–3

Day 5: Amos 1–5

Day 6: Amos 6–9

Day 7: Catch up on any readings you've missed.

GOD SAYS IN JOEL 2:25, "I will give you back what you lost to the swarming locusts, the hopping locusts, the stripping locusts, and the cutting locusts. It was I who sent this great destroying army against you." In this text, we find God extending His grace to the children of Judah. They had just come out of a famine in which all their resources had been devoured. They had gone through a season of loss. And God allowed it because they had done some things that were out of His will. Here God says, *I'm giving back to you all that you lost. I allowed it to be taken, but I'm giving it back.*

We have to remember that when the locusts devoured everything, the nation of Judah had no means of survival. They should have died. But God had a plan to perform a miracle right in their midst. He defied the odds and gave them life again.

In the next verse, God says to Judah, "Once again you will have all the food you want, and you will praise the Lord your God, who does these miracles for you." In other words, *What you're going to receive is going to be so filling that you'll know it's from God.* There have been things in our lives that we thought would destroy us. Our finances took a hit, or our family went through crisis after crisis. But God still had a plan, and in this next season, you're going to see that plan unfold. Thing is, you have to be clear about the season you're in so that you can appreciate the season that's coming.

I know you've had to suffer through some things, but God says that He's going to make it up to you by positioning you to receive more than what you may have lost to the locusts in your life. Yes, it was frustrating, but don't be dismayed—watch God make it up to you! Think of the things you learned while going through the process. The challenges weren't sent to discourage you; they were sent to mature you spiritually and emotionally. They were sent to get your attention and push you into position for this new season. God allowed the losses to make room for what's to come. The losses were great, but the way God is going to make it up to you is going to be worth it all.

POINTS TO PONDER

1. Think of one of the most major losses you've had to endure. How did you handle it?

   _____

   _____

2. Can you say that you have learned any valuable lessons from your season of loss? What were they?

   _____

   _____

3. After your loss, can you see the hand of God moving in any way? If so, in what way? What was your gain?

   _____

   _____

VERSE OF THE WEEK

The Lord says, "I will give you back what you lost to the swarming locusts, the hopping locusts, the stripping locusts, and the cutting locusts. It was I who sent this great destroying army against you. Once again you will have all the food you want, and you will praise the Lord your God, who does these miracles for you. Never again will my people be disgraced. Then you will know that I am among my people Israel, that I am the Lord your God, and there is no other. Never again will my people be disgraced." ▶ **Joel 2:25–27**

WEEK 45
WAITING ON GOD

DAILY READINGS

Day 1: Obadiah 1

Day 2: Jonah 1–4

Day 3: Micah 1–4

Day 4: Micah 5–7

Day 5: Nahum 1–3

Day 6: Habakkuk 1–3

Day 7: Catch up on any readings you've missed.

WAITING IS EASIER said than done. And waiting on God can be particularly difficult. Sometimes His answers are immediate; sometimes He takes His time. Sometimes He allows you to go through a process. We have no control over His timing. We just have to wait until He makes His move.

In Habakkuk 1, we find a prophet who desperately needed to hear from God. He saw the destruction of Judah and called on God for help. Initially, it looked like God wasn't answering or even hearing him. But Habakkuk kept seeking His direction. Has there been anything in your life that you have seriously prayed and sought God for, but you haven't gotten an answer yet?

In this text, Habakkuk asks God two very relevant questions: "How long?" and "Why?" He asks, *How long am I supposed to call for help before you answer? How long am I supposed to put up with these wicked people?* Ladies, you might find yourself asking the same questions over and over: *Why am I still single? Will I ever be financially stable? Will my kids ever listen to me?*

How do we handle it when it feels like God is taking too long? Sometimes we give up. Sometimes we settle for less. Sometimes we take matters into our own hands. When we do any of these things, we disqualify ourselves from receiving the real blessing that He has in store for us. We have to learn to be still and trust God's plan and timing. God knows us better than we know ourselves. He knows what we're prepared for, and He knows when we need a little more time to prepare. He knows the areas where we need growth, and He knows the areas that need a little more discipline. It behooves us to wait, because if we wait on God, He will make sure all of the pieces are perfectly joined together. It will be well worth the wait.

POINTS TO PONDER

1. Think of a time you prayed for God to answer, but He didn't answer the way you wanted Him to. How did you respond?

_____

_____

_____

_____

2. Is there currently something you've been praying about that God has not answered? How long have you been waiting for an answer? What will you do about it now?

_____

_____

_____

_____

3. When God doesn't answer, how do you normally handle His silence?

_____

_____

_____

_____

FURTHER THOUGHTS FOR THE WEEK

In this text, there was a reason why God was delaying an answer. Yes, Judah was God's people, but they had a wicked king who caused them to sin (2 Kings 23:36–37). God had to bring correction to Judah for their wrongdoing, and He used the Babylonians to do it. In the book of Habakkuk, the eponymous prophet goes before the Lord on behalf of the people. We don't know how long he had been calling out to God, but when God spoke, it probably wasn't what Habakkuk wanted to hear. He told the prophet that He was going to allow the Babylonians to raid the land and wage war against Judah. Even though the prophet wasn't seeing God respond in the way and in the timing that he expected, God was still speaking and moving.

THANK GOD FOR GRACE

DAILY READINGS

☐ Day 1: 1 Corinthians 1–4

☐ Day 2: 1 Corinthians 5–8

☐ Day 3: 1 Corinthians 9–12

☐ Day 4: 1 Corinthians 13–16

☐ Day 5: 2 Corinthians 1–6

☐ **Day 6: 2 Corinthians 7–13**

☐ Day 7: Catch up on any readings you've missed.

IN 2 CORINTHIANS 12, Paul talks about being a recipient of God's grace. Paul was once a persecutor of the church, until God changed his life and made him an apostle. In chapter 11, Paul speaks of the trials he has faced as a preacher of the gospel. He's been put in prison, beaten with 39 stripes, and even stoned at one time. He's been shipwrecked three times and left for dead at sea. But even though he's gone through all of those trials, they're nothing compared to his present crisis. This crisis is clearly a serious one, but he doesn't actually mention what it is. Maybe it's something that would cause him embarrassment and humiliation. Maybe it's something that would have ruined his reputation in the church. Whatever it is, he calls it a thorn in his flesh. No matter how much he prays, God won't remove it.

What is that thing that's really bothering you that won't go away and that God won't take away? What is that thing you've been praying about that God won't seem to release you from? What is that thing that makes you cry, and you can't seem to understand why you still have to deal with it? What is your thorn? For some, problems with your children are your thorn. For others, it's your job. Maybe your singleness, the state of your marriage, or your financial situation is your thorn. Whatever it is, you've prayed and cried, but you just can't seem to find any peace. It's hurtful. It's disappointing. It's draining the life out of you.

This is just where Paul was. No matter how much he prayed, God would not remove the thorn. The only thing God would do for Paul was extend him His grace. Paul says that every time he asks the Lord to take it away, God replies, "My grace is all you need" (2 Corinthians 12:9). Some of us have been begging God to help or take away a particular burden, and the only response we've received is that His grace is sufficient. Even when it hurts, His grace has to be enough. I know you want your trial to be over, but the Word of the Lord for you is this: His grace is sufficient.

Because of God's grace, you'll find yourself feeling strengthened when you probably should be falling apart. You'll find yourself laughing at what used to make you cry. If, because of God's grace, you still have a roof over your head, food on the table, and many other blessings that He loads you with daily, thank God for His grace!

POINTS TO PONDER

1. What is your personal definition of grace?

_____

_____

_____

_____

2. Do you have a thorn in your flesh? What is your thorn?

_____

_____

_____

_____

3. What do you do when you've prayed and God doesn't respond the way you want Him to? How do you handle it?

_____

_____

_____

_____

THIS IS MY PRAYER

Dear Lord,
Please help me accept the things that I cannot change. Help me accept Your will in every area of my life. I trust Your Word that when I am weak, that's when I am strongest, because I am relying on You alone to be my strength. I understand that Your grace is enough; therefore, I am relying on Your grace to keep me and sustain me in the days, weeks, and months to come. In Jesus's name, amen.

EXPECT IT, SEE IT, ACHIEVE IT

DAILY READINGS

- Day 1: Zephaniah 1–3
- **Day 2: Haggai 1–2**
- Day 3: Zechariah 1–5
- Day 4: Zechariah 6–10
- Day 5: Zechariah 11–14
- Day 6: Malachi 1–4
- Day 7: Catch up on any readings you've missed.

LET'S TALK ABOUT EXPECTANCY for a moment. A woman who is pregnant knows that there is a life growing inside her. She knows that at the set time, that which she is expecting will come forth. There is no doubt in her mind, because she sees and feels the growth. Her body has changed, her mind-set has changed, and as time goes on, her level of expectancy changes, because she knows that any day now, new birth will come forth and her life will change forever.

That's how we have to be, too. If we're going to reach greater things, our expectancy has to grow to the point where we know God is going to help us accomplish what we can't yet comprehend or imagine. You may not know all God has in store for you, but you've got to expect Him to do great things through you. In fact, you have to believe it to the point that you can envision it before you actually see it. You have to envision it, and then position yourself to accomplish whatever those goals are.

In the book of Haggai, this was the message that God was trying to relay to the nation of Judah. They were at a place where they were positioned to move forward. They had rebuilt the temple, but they feared it didn't match the beauty of the first one. When Solomon built the first temple, he spared no expense in material and laborers. What they saw before them now didn't have the splendor of what they had seen before. They were comparing their present to their past.

Sometimes we're the same way. Sometimes we limit ourselves because of our age, our gender, our physical abilities—the list goes on. We see our flaws, and we can't see ourselves on a higher level. We compare ourselves to those we see on television or social media. We compare our gifts and gauge our abilities against theirs. We tell ourselves that we're not beautiful or educated enough. We doubt ourselves and place limitations upon ourselves, because we think we're not up to par.

Please be encouraged and know that there's nothing you can't achieve when God is with you. You've got to be willing to put in the work, to stretch yourself in order to achieve that ministry position, elected office, or next career level. Just as God promised Haggai, He's going to be with you every step of the way. Please know, my dear sister, that there is more to you than meets the eye. There is greatness in you, and God is going to do amazing work through you. Don't compare yourself to others. You are exactly who God wants you to be. Just position yourself for Him to do even greater things through you. Expect it, see it, and you will achieve it.

POINTS TO PONDER

1. How do you see yourself: average, great, or neither? Why?

_____

_____

_____

_____

2. Do you have high expectations for yourself, your family, and/or your career? If so, what are those expectations? If not, why?

_____

_____

_____

_____

3. Have you ever found yourself comparing your abilities to those of others? How did that help or hinder you?

THIS IS MY PRAYER

Dear Lord,

I acknowledge that You are Lord of all. You are the Lord of my past, present, and future. I trust Your plans for me. I trust that You know what's best for me. Help me not be distracted or hindered in any way, but help me remain excited and in expectation of the plans that You have for my future. Help me see myself as You see me. For You are a great God, and I am expecting You to do great things through me. In Jesus's name, amen.

WEEK 48
GETTING BACK
TO WHERE I WAS

DAILY READINGS

- [ ] Day 1: Ezra 1–5
- [ ] Day 2: Ezra 6–10
- [ ] Day 3: Nehemiah 1–3
- [ ] **Day 4: Nehemiah 4–7**
- [ ] Day 5: Nehemiah 8–10
- [ ] Day 6: Nehemiah 11–13
- [ ] Day 7: Catch up on any readings you've missed.

THE BOOK OF NEHEMIAH comes on the heels of the Jews' return to Jerusalem after the Babylonian exile ended. But while hundreds of men were rebuilding the wall around Jerusalem and guarding against attacks from their enemies, their home life was in jeopardy: A famine had hit so hard that they had to mortgage their land just to get food for their families. The problem was that the nobles and officials lending them the money would charge them a high interest rate, and many of the men had to sell their children into slavery to pay off the debt.

Even when you're doing the work of the Lord, life still happens. The enemy couldn't get them one way, but he sure found a way in. He attacked their families. That's how the enemy is. If he can't get you one way, he'll get you another. The key is in how you handle the attack.

Nehemiah 5:1 says there was an outcry, and the men and their wives began to share their problems with Nehemiah. They cared enough about their families and their homes to fight on their behalf. They weren't afraid to tell Nehemiah what they needed. They didn't just accept what was going on. They had been putting their time in on that wall for the good of everyone—surely that had to count for something. So they got up the nerve to tell the truth and ask for what seemed to be the hard thing.

We all have to get to the place where we stop hiding behind the mask and tell the truth. If you're hurt, say you're hurt. If you're having a hard time making ends meet, say you're having a hard time making ends meet. Be honest with yourself and with God. Many of us have gotten off track and lost our focus. Many of us have lost some of ourselves because we've been pulled in other directions. We've lost our zeal. We've lost a little of our peace. We might have even lost the desire to persevere. Now be honest and tell God what you want. Tell Him your heart's desire. Don't be afraid to ask God for the hard thing. James 4:2 says, "You do not have, because you do not ask" (ESV). If we're going to get where we need to be, we can't be afraid to ask for it. God wants to bring about restoration in our lives, but we have to have an honest moment with ourselves, then trust God to do what no other power is able to do.

~~~~~~

POINTS TO PONDER

1. Life happens to all of us, but what is one personal thing that fell through the cracks for you while you were focused on doing something for others?

   _____

   _____

   _____

   _____

2. When you feel you're under spiritual attack, how do you handle it? Who do you talk to about it?

   _____

   _____

   _____

   _____

3. If there were one thing you could ask God to restore for you personally, what would that be? Why?

   _____

   _____

   _____

   _____

VERSE OF THE WEEK

"You must restore their fields, vineyards, olive groves, and homes to them this very day. And repay the interest you charged when you lent them money, grain, new wine, and olive oil."

They replied, "We will give back everything and demand nothing more from the people. We will do as you say." Then I called the priests and made the nobles and officials swear to do what they had promised. ▸Nehemiah 5:11–12

GO FOR IT!

DAILY READINGS

Day 1: Galatians 1–6

Day 2: Ephesians 1–6

Day 3: Philippians 1–4

Day 4: Colossians 1–4

Day 5: 1 Thessalonians 1–5

Day 6: 2 Thessalonians 1–3

Day 7: Catch up on any readings you've missed.

I THINK IT'S SAFE TO SAY that we're often our own worst enemy. We can talk ourselves out of anything. We can quickly come up with an excuse for why we can't do something or go somewhere. We can allow our insecurities and shortcomings to overcome us. But sometimes you have to tell your fears and anxieties to take a backseat and just go for it! Go pursue your dreams for your home or your vision for your business. Don't settle where you are, just go for it!

In Philippians 3:12, Paul writes about deciding on his next move in life. He realized that he had not arrived at the destination he desired. He had not accomplished all that God had for him to accomplish. Although he had come a long way, he still had a long way to go. So he said he'd forget those things that were behind him and press on (Philippians 3:13). He was going for it.

Paul was a very intelligent man. He realized that his past did not define him. He realized that he couldn't get bogged down with all he'd done in his past. He realized that it did him no good to get sidetracked by the enemies he made—but by the same token, he couldn't get all caught up in his accomplishments, either. He understood that it wasn't about where he was or where he had been. It was all about where he was going.

We have to take a lesson from Paul's experience and admit that sometimes we get overwhelmed by thoughts from our past. We can get caught up in what used to be. We can't move forward in our careers or our relationships with family and friends, because we're too busy grieving over past hurts. However, this next move is not about where you've been. This next move is not about the mistakes. This next move is about where you're going.

We have the potential to do great things. There is something greater than you can see or comprehend right now. When God begins to reveal His plan, we can't hesitate. We have to be ready to just go for it. So don't get bogged down by your past. Don't allow your fears to hold you back. You have people who are assigned to your life, and they are waiting on what has to come through you. So no more delays, no more excuses, no more distractions. Just go for it!

POINTS TO PONDER

1. What is a goal or dream that you have talked yourself out of, and why?

_____

_____

_____

_____

2. What group of people is assigned to your life? In what way do you impact their lives the most?

_____

_____

_____

_____

3. How has your past influenced or affected your potential future?

_____

_____

_____

_____

ACTIONS FOR THE WEEK

1. Write a list of at least three goals or dreams and begin to develop a vision for them.

2. Begin to work on a strategy to bring those dreams and goals to fruition.

3. Write a list of hindrances that you will denounce daily (e.g., fear, doubt, slothfulness) until those things are no longer a significant part of your life.

WEEK 50
USE YOUR GIFT

DAILY READINGS

Day 1: 1 Timothy 1–6

Day 2: 2 Timothy 1–4

Day 3: Titus 1–3

Day 4: Philemon 1

Day 5: 1 Peter 1–5

Day 6: 2 Peter 1–3

Day 7: Catch up on any readings you've missed.

EVERYTHING IN LIFE has a purpose. Everyone on this planet was born with and for a purpose. In his book *In Pursuit of Purpose*, Myles Munroe writes that "without purpose, life has no meaning." He says that "in the absence of purpose, time has no meaning, energy has no reason, and life has no precision." Therefore, it's vital that we all learn what our purpose is so that our lives will be fulfilled and complete.

Every person and every gift plays a part within the body of Christ. I've found that the best way to discover your purpose is by using your gifts. Sometimes something may not even seem like a gift to you because you do it so naturally, but everyone has something they have been gifted to do. Paul said it like this in Romans 12:6–8: "In his grace, God has given us different gifts for doing certain things well. . . . If your gift is serving others, serve them well. If you are a teacher, teach well. If your gift is to encourage others, be encouraging. If it is giving, give generously." In other words, whatever gift God has given you, use it gladly, to the best of your ability, and for the glory of God.

God equips and enables us with the necessary tools to carry out His plan and complete the purpose He has designed for our lives. Sometimes we take those things for granted because they seem simple. Believe it or not, those simple things that we take lightly or don't see as gifts are often the very things that let us encourage, help, and add value to others' lives. What am I talking about? Peter says that we are first to love each other, then be hospitable toward each other, then use our gifts to minister to each other. Those things may seem to be common, ordinary acts of kindness, but for those who extend this kindness, it's actually their purpose.

Everyone has an ability that can only come from God and that is the basis of their purpose on earth. Whatever you do, know that God will give you the strength and ability to get it done. You may not have the same talent that others have. But, my dear sister, never doubt that you are needed. You and all you bring to the table are a part of God's divine purpose. Your gifts, your beautiful smile, the love that you give, your genuine kindness and hospitality—it's all for His divine purpose.

POINTS TO PONDER

1. Have you discovered what you are gifted to do? What are your gifts?

    _____

    _____

2. Do you know what your purpose in life is? What is it?

    _____

    _____

3. What event(s) can you recall that may have contributed to the manifestation of your purpose?

    _____

    _____

VERSE OF THE WEEK

God has given each of you a gift from his great variety of spiritual gifts. Use them well to serve one another. Do you have the gift of speaking? Then speak as though God himself were speaking through you. Do you have the gift of helping others? Do it with all the strength and energy that God supplies. Then everything you do will bring glory to God through Jesus Christ. All glory and power to him forever and ever! Amen. ▶ **1 Peter 4:10–11**

IF YOU LOVE HIM, PROVE IT

DAILY READINGS

Day 1: Hebrews 1–7

Day 2: Hebrews 8–13

Day 3: James 1–5

Day 4: 1 John 1–5

Day 5: 2 John 1, 3 John 1

Day 6: Jude 1

Day 7: Catch up on any readings you've missed.

IN HIS BOOK *The 5 Love Languages*, Gary Chapman says everybody has a certain "love language" they use to express love and interpret how others give them love. Some of us need quality time; others need to feel the touch of another. Some need words of affirmation, some love to receive gifts, and some of us get excited about acts of service like mowing the lawn or picking the laundry up from the cleaners. *Agape*—a Greek word for the highest form of love, the kind God shows to us—allows us to love even when we don't feel like we're being loved. When we have an *agape* love, we give to others even though we may not receive. We show kindness even when kindness is not shown to us. We love others even when that love is not reciprocated. It's not always easy, but it is doable with the help of the Holy Spirit and the love of God that we have inside us.

For example, we say we love God, but we don't always show it, perhaps because we take for granted that He knows our hearts. Yes, He knows our thoughts and intentions, but it is His desire that we show it. If we say we love Him, He wants us to prove it. Isn't that what He did when He sent His Son to die for our sins? No, He's not asking us to give our firstborn, but I believe there are things we can do to prove our love for Him.

This is the sentiment that John is stressing to his readers in 1 John 4. If we say we love God, we've got to do more than just talk about it; we've got to show it in our actions. Love is not just a feeling; it's an action. And we have to show the love we have for God tangibly, by loving and serving others. In other words, our love for God is displayed through our actions toward each other.

John tells us that one way we can show that we love the Father

is to love His children, too. Remember, He is the one who determines who our other "family members" are, not us. We are simply called to accept them and love them as His own. We are not to judge whether they're His or not. Whether or not they look like us or act like us, we still have to show them love, because they're a part of the family of God. If you love God, then prove it by loving His children, too.

POINTS TO PONDER

1. What's your love language?

_____

_____

2. How difficult or easy is it for you to show love to others who don't show love to you?

_____

_____

3. How have you proven your love to God lately?

_____

_____

VERSE OF THE WEEK

If anyone says, "I love God," and hates his brother, he is a liar; for he who does not love his brother whom he has seen cannot love God whom he has not seen. ▶ 1 John 4:20 (ESV)

WEEK 52
ACCESS GRANTED

DAILY READINGS

Day 1: Revelation 1–3

Day 2: Revelation 4–7

Day 3: Revelation 8–11

Day 4: Revelation 12–15

Day 5: Revelation 16–19

Day 6: Revelation 20–22

Day 7: Catch up on any readings you've missed.

IN REVELATION 3:8, John spoke to the church in Philadelphia and quoted Jesus, saying, "I know all the things you do, and I have opened a door for you that no one can close." In other words, *I've given you access. I've made it possible for you to lay claim to what has been promised to you.* But why Philadelphia? Of the seven churches of Asia Minor, why was this the only one that did not receive a rebuke about anything in Revelation? Instead of correction, they received a blessing.

You see, this church had a level of commitment that the other churches didn't have. Because of their faithfulness, because they had successfully reached out to the lost, God gave them access that could not be denied by anyone. But before He told them about the open door, He introduced Himself as "the one who is holy and true, the one who has the key of David. What he opens, no one can close; and what he closes, no one can open" (Revelation 3:7). God already has the keys to death, hell, and the grave (not to mention the keys to the kingdom)—now He announces to the church that He has the keys to our future, finances, and careers. It's a blessed assurance to know who holds the keys.

We're so busy trying to make the right connections and get in the right doors. But at the end of the day, no one on earth even holds all the keys—only God does. When we're faithful to God, He is faithful to us. He's the kind of God who can put your name before the right people or give you favor in places where you least expect it. If anyone tries to shut the door that He's opened, they won't be able to do it, because He holds the keys. He has the power to open doors no human can shut and to shut doors no human can open.

Now, there will be some doors God won't open for you, because they don't fit His plan. But that's because He has a better door prepared for you. So don't get weary when doors begin to shut. Get excited that our God has given us access to what no eyes have seen and no ears have heard. Get excited about the door that He *has* given you access to, the door that is so much greater than what we can imagine.

POINTS TO PONDER

1. Have you ever bemoaned a door that seemed closed to you? Could you see God in it in any way?

_____

_____

_____

_____

2. If you had a choice to obtain the keys to walk through any door you desired, which door would you want access to (e.g., healing, financial freedom, career)?

_____

_____

_____

_____

3. If you could permanently close a door, which would you choose (e.g., job, relationship, the past), and why?

_____

_____

_____

_____

VERSE OF THE WEEK

Write this letter to the angel of the church in Philadelphia.

This is the message from the one who is holy and true, the one who has the key of David. What he opens, no one can close; and what he closes, no one can open:

I know all the things you do, and I have opened a door for you that no one can close. You have little strength, yet you obeyed my word and did not deny me. ▸ Revelation 3:7–8

GROUP STUDY GUIDE

1. Go around the room and allow each person to share their favorite chapter and/or verse from the week's readings.

2. How do you interpret this particular text? What do you hear the author saying?

3. Are there any companion scriptures that you know will complement this text?

4. As you read the text, do you see more of God's love, His mercy, or His anger? Explain.

5. How can this text be applied to your life?

6. Can you identify with any particular character within the text? Can you see yourself in this text in any way?

7. After reading the weekly commentary, what will you do differently as you go forward?

8. How have this week's readings encouraged you to do better and be better?

9. After reading the scripture and commentary, what principles have you acquired that you might teach others?

10. After reading the text, take a moment to encourage the person sitting next to you based upon something you have read in the text.

RESOURCES

"An Easy Step-by-Step Method of Studying the Bible"
Mary Fairchild
This is a great seven-step method of studying the Bible. You can access the article online at https://www.learnreligions.com/how-to-study-the-bible-700238.

NLT Life Application Study Bible
This Bible is super easy to understand, and reading it just makes you want to read more. The scripture itself is the New Living Translation, which uses a tone and vocabulary that is familiar to modern readers. The annotations help readers understand the culture and traditions of biblical times.

HarperCollins Bible Commentary, Revised Edition
James L. Mays (ed.)
This commentary gives amazing insight into and interpretation of the biblical text. It's a good source to use when you want an overall commentary on the individual books of the Bible.

HarperCollins Study Bible
Revised and updated by Harold W. Attridge
This Bible gives us a wealth of historical background data and outlines. It also comes with its own commentary to give the reader greater insight while reading.

NKJV Woman's Study Bible: Receiving God's Truth for Balance, Hope, and Transformation

Dorothy Kelley Patterson and Rhonda Harrington Kelley (eds.)

In this study Bible for women, you'll find features throughout the text that have been designed to speak to a woman's heart. It also contains contributions by women leaders from a variety of ethnic, denominational, educational, and occupational backgrounds.

REFERENCES

Chapman, Gary. *The 5 Love Languages: The Secret to Love That Lasts*. Chicago: Northfield Publishing, 1992.

Munroe, Myles. *In Pursuit of Purpose: The Key to Personal Fulfillment*. Shippensburg, PA: Destiny Image, 1992.

INDEX

Purpose
  as found by using your
    gifts, 175–176
  God's plan for individuals, 13, 25,
    107, 135–136, 142
  helping others fulfill purpose,
    11–12, 18, 105, 138
  of Mary the anointer, 104
In Pursuit of Purpose (Munroe), 175

R
Rachel, 7, 8

S
Samuel, 55, 57
Sarah, 3
Satan, 75, 87, 96, 97
Saul, King, 63
Shadrach, 145
Sin
  forgiveness of, 82, 84, 115
  Jesus, as sacrificed for our sins,
    111, 178
  nation of Judah persisting in,
    132, 157
  personal sins, God allowing us
    to see, 114
  unintentional sin, 21
Solomon, King, 84, 107, 163
Spiritual rut, expanding
    beyond, 120–121
Stress, 15–16, 55–56

T
Transition, meeting the challenges
    of, 39–41
Trust
  in God's plan for your life, 97, 118,
    130, 165
  in the grace of God, 128
  as increased by speaking
    positively, 5
  during periods of wait, 56,
    78–79
  in the power of God, 168
  prayer for bolstering trust, 13
  strength, given to those who
    trust, 81–82
  succeeding against the
    odds, 50
  in timing of God, 107
  in track record of God, 53
  victory, trust in God
    leading to, 59
  in the Word of God, 4

U
Uzzah (son of Abinadab), 59, 81
Uzziah, King, 114

X
Xerxes, King, 93, 94

Z
Zelophehad, daughters of, 36

ACKNOWLEDGMENTS

I have to thank the good Lord above for giving me an understanding of His Word that I can apply to my life and use to develop sermons and teaching sessions to deliver to others. I would also like to thank the congregation of Emmanuel Missionary Baptist Church, where I am blessed to serve as senior pastor, for allowing me the opportunity to share God's Word with you on a weekly basis.

ABOUT THE AUTHOR

 **Dr. Kimberly D. Moore, DMin,** is the senior pastor of Emmanuel Missionary Baptist Church in Gastonia, North Carolina, and the founder of Kimberly Moore Ministries, a nonprofit outreach ministry that aims to empower others through classes, mentoring sessions, and scholarships. She is a graduate of Gardner-Webb University School of Divinity, where she received a master of divinity degree and a doctor of ministry degree in pastoral ministries. Additionally, Dr. Moore is an itinerant minister who has been blessed to travel sharing the gospel of Jesus Christ. She gives God all the glory for the favor that is upon her life.